DESIGNING THE

Marriage

YOU DESERVE

FROM ONE WIFE TO ANOTHER

Designing The Marriage You Deserve
From One Wife To Another

ISBN: 978-1-7365129-8-2

10 9 8 7 6 5 4 3 2 1
Printed in the United States

Priceless Publishing®
Coral Springs, Fl
www.pricelesspublishing.co

Dedication

I'd like to dedicate this book to the couple who showed me what marriage could be if you worked at it. My grandparents were not just married for 57 years before my grandfather passed, but loved each other until the end. I'm grateful to have witnessed that expression of love up close for most of my life, a lot of my playbook comes from them.

To the love of my life, thank you for believing in me, cheering for me, and loving me more than I thought possible. You make me feel like the best thing since sliced bread LOL. You+Me forever!

Mommy, one of my life goals has been and will always be to make you proud. I hope I'm doing my job!

Saxon and Syon, I pray this shows you two that dreams can come true if you make a plan and work at it. Mommy loves you!

Contents

Introduction

WHO YOU WERE VS. WHO YOU ARE

Hello Mrs. or soon-to-be Mrs.

How are you?

I'm not sure what made you grab this book or even open to the first page, but I pray I'm able to impart some wisdom and leave you feeling like a slightly better version of yourself than you were before reading this book. When you see or hear the word, 'Marriage,' what do you think of? Do you immediately envision a gorgeous wedding day? A lifetime of happiness? A lifetime of settling? What is your visualization of marriage? If you're already married, is your marriage living up to what you thought it would before you got married? If not, why? If yes, great! But can it get better? The answer is if you want it!

This book is not about how to get the best Marriage ever real quick just by reading. Sorry (not sorry). This book is for the woman who knows that greatness is on the other side of work and is willing to put in the great work to reap the results she wants. When we're just floating through life, not really putting in the effort to go after the things we desire, it's almost as if life is happening to us. It is up to us to get up, figure out what we want, reign in the strings, and make a mark in this life. We have one life to live, and the good news is, we have the responsibility of designing it the best way. To achieve that, we have to decide on what we actually want and consciously go after it.

What if I tell you that many of our ideals of Marriage are what we saw or didn't see growing up? Shocker right? Sometimes unknowingly, we'll expect our spouse to show up just like our dads (and in some cases nothing like our dads), moms, and grandmas. That is a disaster waiting to happen for a few reasons. Even if your mom and dad have been married for 30+ years and you desire a marriage that embodies theirs, you and your husband are not them. What worked for them may not work for you and your husband in the same way because you are not the same people. No person in this world is identical to you or your husband (even if you are an identical twin).

No two people have ever lived your love story before, and that is why it is your love story to create. Not mom, dad, Clair & Cliff Huxtable, or any other couple you admire have a perfect Marriage (please believe every single couple has a portion of their story you wouldn't want to share). We also need to realize that what we've commonly seen in relationships generations ago was not necessarily the loving marriage we want to strive for today. In many marriages of ages past, they stayed married for many years for reasons outside of love. So while they showed us that we have to remain in the marriage, they didn't necessarily show us or tell us *how* to stay and be happy? Staying in a marriage because you want to stay and being in a marriage because you're happy and fulfilled are two different things.

Many marriages of the past lasted because they didn't have a choice. The result is, many people were married for a long time and in a loveless marriage for a long time. Not because they wanted to be in a loveless marriage, but because people didn't talk about the inner workings of other people's marriages, nor did people subscribe to the idea that they could or should live out a storybook romance. People stayed for the business of Marriage. He works; I don't. The kids need both of us. I don't have enough money to make it on my own, and the list goes on. None of those reasons was wrong. They did the best they could with what they had. The thing is, we have access to so much more, so my expectation for today's woman is to use what we've got to not only want better but achieve better!

I hope that the women of our generation don't just stay to stay and say they are married, but that we stay because although Marriage is work and sometimes challenging, it is rewarding because, we are happy, healthy, loved, and whole. Happiness doesn't just happen. Happiness doesn't just fall into your lap when you're single, so throw in an additional person with different emotions, hard-wired thinking, and needs. Happiness won't be knocking you upside your head every morning just because you want to be happy. Your husband's nuclear family has shaped him up until this point, in the same way your nuclear family has shaped you. Because you come from two different nuclear families, getting you both on the same page will take some effort. You probably think it didn't take any effort in the beginning. Whelp, there is a scientific explanation for that.

Gary Chapman, the famous author, and psychologist behind the five love languages, explains that there are endorphins that we experience in the beginning phases and excitement of lusting after someone. These are sometimes called the *"happy hormone."* He explains that this can last about a year or so before we start to come down from that natural height and settle into real life. As that happens, it is easier to pick up on all the quirks and annoying habits that were easy to ignore before. Now that you're married and facing the realities thereof, you're going to have to work for the results that those *"happy hormones"* naturally provided before. Happiness is something we have to pursue when life is happening to us. Don't intertwine happiness with joy.

Your joy is on the inside and shouldn't be able to be blown back and forth by anybody. This world didn't give it, and it can't take it! We don't just wake up with a person who is different from us and magically fall into happiness every day (unless you're on a romantic vacation, where real-life does not reside, lol). Happiness in a long-lasting marriage is attainable. We just have first to be clear of the goal and then intentionally go after it. Living in a state of happiness will require research, thinking, time, communication, and guessing it works on our part. In today's overly saturated social media world, it's easy to begin to covet other people's lives (please be careful with that y'all). Dig into what is essential for you.

Do you see a theme here? We need to be personalizing our marriages to fit us. It's not a one size fit for all kinds of situations. Check yourself first, turn off the noise of all outside influences, and ask yourself what you want out of your Marriage. Then check in with your husband. I firmly believe marriage is what we make it; we get out of it what we put into it. As a Christian, I know that Marriage is important to God for many reasons. Since it is important to Him and He is nothing but goodness, Marriage should be as you guessed it. Goodness! Not to say that it will be good 100% of the time (we're human, and our husbands will get on our nerves and vice versa), but it should be overwhelmingly sweet and fruitful (not just in a multiplying way).

You should be experiencing growth, happiness, fulfillment, love, connection and this list goes on from your Marriage. We aren't living in a fictional romance novel, so of course, we'll experience ups and downs. However, the good should far outweigh the bad. If you aren't experiencing what you would consider a "great" marriage, the good news is it's not too late. You can begin where you are with what you have. I don't know about you, but I didn't get married to experience mediocre love or life. A big part of having the Marriage you like is being the person you desire. If you're showing up as anyone else, you're going to request and choose things that the real you don't treasure or even want.

We have to show up as the most authentic versions of ourselves in our marriages. If no other person deserves to see the completeness in us, flaws and all, it's our husbands. How can they help us reach our best potential if we're hiding parts of who we are from them? It's beneficial to you, your husband, and the Marriage when you let your guard down and let him into who you are. And if you're thinking, I don't really know who I am, and you aren't alone. A lot of women, including myself, are trying to figure out who we are really. The key is, as you figure it out, let it be known. Be vocal about discovering your likes and dislikes, dreams and desires. Allow your husband to support you in this road of discovery.

As women, we throw ourselves into being the best wife we can be and forget about the woman we dreamt of being before we said I do. I have a secret for you, though. The more discovering you do, the more you'll become aware of what you need and what's important to you. The closer you become to the woman you want to be, the better you'll feel. The better you feel about yourself, the happier you are, the better you are for everyone else. Not the secret you were looking for? It's legit the secret sauce though! Think about when you get dressed in something fly and put on some makeup. Don't you just feel like you're exuding excellence? or owning the day? Everything just flows and works better when you feel good about yourself. If you're going to go after the Marriage, you want the actual work to start with who you see in the mirror, whom you show up as yourself. Who is she? What does she want? What does she like? In this book, I want us to walk together through going after the marriage you deserve and desire, but better yet, the union that God wants for you.

When we show up as the best versions of ourselves for our marriages and ultimately our families, everybody wins! Another big part of the puzzle is appreciating the gift that is your spouse. Yes, I said gift, let that simmer lol (I know, I know we're the real gift, but we'll get into all of that). Think about how we treat gifts that we treasure. We keep them in a safe place, we admire them often, we appreciate them. We have to have that same posture with our marriages and husbands. They are gifts and aren't easily replaceable so let's treat them with the same excitement we had for them when we were only dreaming of them.

I know it sounds a lot easier than it is lol, but that's why we're walking through this book. Grab a glass of something yummy (depending on the time of day, it's coffee or wine for me), your favorite snack, and cuddle up with a cozy blanket. Let's dive in!

Words From A Wise Wife

"Develop and pursue your interests, along with those you develop as a couple. Have fun together!"

-Dr. Frances "Toni" Draper
Pastor of Freedom Temple AME Zion Church
Author of No Ordinary Hookup: The Courtship
of Vashti and Carl Murphy (1915-1916)
Married 47 years

Reflection

1. What do you love about yourself? Revisit this list often and affirm yourself!

_____

_____

_____

_____

_____

_____

2. What do you enjoy for fun? List it here and make it a thing! Do these things more often.

_____

_____

_____

_____

_____

_____

3. What makes you laugh? List it here and do more of that!

_____

_____

_____

_____

_____

_____

_____

_____

4. How do you recharge yourself? List it here, and then put your charging sessions on the calendar.

_____

_____

_____

_____

_____

_____

_____

_____

5. When was the last time you felt like you didn't want the activity you were doing to end? Figure out a time to do this thing again!

_____

_____

_____

_____

_____

_____

_____

_____

6. Who do you want to show up as for yourself? Aside from your roles to your husband and children?

_____

_____

_____

_____

_____

_____

_____

_____

Words From A Wise Wife

"You cannot unsay anything, just like you cannot unhear anything. For that reason, be mindful that every word spoken to & about your husband/Marriage becomes a thread in your family's tapestry. Take a look; what pattern do you see? Wives, let us remember Proverbs 12:18."

-Chaplain Yolanda Compton
Marriage and Family Therapist
Married 28 years

Designing The Marriage

THAT SERVES YOU

For many of us, including myself, we were a Ms. longer than we've been a Mrs. We probably know that Ms. Inside and out. Favorite color, favorite music, what makes her tick, and what sets her off (depending on when you got married, you may still have work to do in uncovering yourself). We've loved her, nurtured her, had standards and goals for her. She was all we knew, and we knew her well (hopefully)... Many adult women of a certain age are so focused on becoming a Mrs. That they forget to nurture that Ms. and ladies. If you happen to be reading this and not married yet, please don't make that mistake. That person deserves to be cared for, no matter the stage. Nothing comes before it's time, you have the rest of your life to be married and just a season of singleness, enjoy it!! Trust me, there will come a time when you look back to your single-hood with nostalgia. How do I know?

I was that single girl. I had a boyfriend (now my husband) since college. I have been checking my personal goals off the list while attempting to be a good friend, girlfriend, daughter, sister, etc. Once all my personal goals were crossed off my list, I was ready (so I thought) for that excellent, big title. Sign me up for the role of a wife! I've gone to school, gotten a good job, held down my apartment.

I'm ready, I thought. Now being a Mrs. for 8 years, I laugh at that girl. She was not prepared! Thank God my husband waited until he was ready to propose.

Our marriage is sweeter because of it. Had I got my way?! Whew, thank God for Jesus. I digress. Things were pretty simple back then. Most of the responsibilities I now carry were merely thoughts (if that) back then. There is no way that a mid-twenty-year-old girl could handle all that this 30-year-old is doing now. I simply wasn't ready. And if we aren't careful, we miss out on the sweetness of what currently is by obsessing over what is not ours yet. Enjoy each season you find yourself in. The more secure you are when you get married, the easier it will be to give yourself to marriage fully. Society and we sometimes think that when we get married, we have to come second and abandon the girl we were to the Mrs. we are now in our marriage? I'm not saying that we shouldn't want to give the best of ourselves to our husbands (and children, if you have any).

What I'm saying is, we can end up giving from a place of lack if we forget all about the girl inside who is so much of who we are. The girl that we tend to forget about and leave behind is the girl who attracted your husband to you. How can we get married and then decide she's no longer the star of the show or, worse, no longer important? I'm sure you've heard this before, but you give your best when you're at your best. When you're flying with children, the flight attendants always tell you, put your mask on first. That is because if you aren't getting any oxygen, how can you be of optimal assistance to anyone else? You're of no help to anyone else if you're dying (literally or figuratively).

So I know it sounds so easy, right? Just take care of yourself, do things to feed your soul every day, right? Lol, umm, hmmm, I hear you now, easier said than done. You're probably asking yourself where even to begin. I'm glad you asked. First of all, it takes a real honest look at yourself and where you stand now. I hope you did the work page before this chapter. Start asking yourself those questions. What do you enjoy? Who are you now? What parts of that Mrs. do you want to bring into this season of your life? What versions of her no longer serve you? Begin to cut out some time for yourself, do not only scroll social media, but scroll yourself and your heart too. What's in there? What is your heart saying? Hopefully, you have been thinking about these questions.

I've recently started to do this in my own life. I realized that amidst the Covid-19 crisis, I needed something for myself. It was effortless to get caught up in all things at home, life and never give myself a minute of alone time. If I'm honest, I thought it was selfish and a bit mean to say I needed some alone time. We had a brand new baby at the beginning of the pandemic. Who did I think I was to say I needed a break from my family and all of this new responsibility? Well, who I was turning into was someone unpleasant to be around because I felt stifled. I realized I needed to do something different. The life loop I was living was starting to deplete me. I realized it was up to me to change if I didn't like what I was doing.

So I started with getting up a little earlier in the morning to have some quiet time before the house turned up. This was crucial to me. It's currently the only time of the day I really have to sit alone with my thoughts (morning time is how this book was written, lol). It allowed me time to think about what I enjoyed that I wasn't doing. How could I add those things back to my life? I enjoy spa time. In the midst of life living (yes, I know it's not a real word, lol), how can I, a mother of two small children and wife and friend and employee and author, find the time to go sit and be *"pampered"* for an hour or more? I put pampered in quotes because, to me, spa time is way more than time just to be pampered. It is literally replenishing for me, life-giving. I use it as a time to pray, meditate and hydrate areas of my mind that I haven't had time to give water to in a long time.

When I break it down in that matter, it's almost a no-brainer that I would make time to go more often than not, but the key is I have to do it so that it does not become a burden to my spouse. I never want what I need to become something that takes away from him because it will no longer feel good to me. It will become like a guilty pleasure, and nothing I'm doing to better myself or pour into myself should feel guilty. Once I identified this was something I needed, I communicated it to him. Then I had to follow through with keeping that appointment with myself. I don't know about you, but sometimes I have a hard time committing things to my schedule if I feel like they will cause interference with my regularly scheduled program.

Let me stop right here and say that's okay. I'm a planner at heart, and I like things to fall neatly into place. With the work of my therapist (get you one). If *"the regularly scheduled program"* no longer serves you, it's okay to change it. The schedule should be an outline, not a hard unchangeable requirement. Put that new thing on the calendar, and do it. Whatever will aid you in feeling good about yourself and your life is worth it. We can't prioritize meetings and appointments with everyone else but ourselves. We should be on our own calendars. I hope you all are following me through this example. Replace spa with anything you like to do for yourself (going to the coffee shop for a couple of hours on Saturday morning to read, mani/Pedi appointments, whatever breathes life into you).

You have to identify that thing first. Then communicate to your spouse what your thing is and how it enables you to tap into the best version of yourself. Then you communicate what support from them looks like for you to be free to pour into yourself for a few hours a month, a week, or whatever works for the life you two are living. If what makes you tick requires daily time alone, you could incorporate that without imposing on your spouse by waking up earlier than them or staying up later than them. That would require you to figure out what part of the day you thrive. If waking up earlier than your spouse sounds like a nightmare and you would spend most of that time being groggy, or you wouldn't be able to commit to that, try staying up after they go to bed.

The goal here is to get time to yourself when you can turn off outside distractions to do something that is important to you. That could be reading, adult coloring, writing, Bible study, journaling, whatever that thing is, figure it out. Just because we have joined with another person to conquer life, it does not mean you should have no alone time or no time to enjoy what makes you happy. Your spouse married you because you were YOU. So completely changing or morphing into some new version of yourself, who forgets the very person you are probably isn't what he's looking for. All of this work requires a real, honest self-assessment. Set aside the time to do it. It's so, so important.

Now I'm in no way saying that you should not be evolving. As I stated above, there will be things from your season of singleness that no longer serve you, and that's okay, it is expected.

The Merriam-Webster dictionary

defines change as follows:

to alter, vary, modify to make or become different.

Many people have a negative connotation associated with people changing due to an outlier (college, sorority, new job, and just go on ahead and add Marriage to that list).

I'm not sure why people think so negatively around change because, frankly, I desire to be a different, better version every single day! Who wants to be the same woman at 18 and 28 or 38?

If I paid for a degree and at the end of the program I wasn't any more intelligent or different, I would want a refund. Most people enroll in a higher educational program to improve their understanding of a particular topic. With that improved knowledge, you are growing, and you guessed it is changing. Some aspects of life are meant to alter you. If I was still acting like the person I was then, now we'd have a huge problem. Change can be a positive thing and should be embraced. Not all seasons in life require the same thing out of us, and some modifications come with the wisdom only time can give. If you've ever heard someone say about you, *"oh, she's changed,"* you should feel good about that. Embrace it. If you've changed for the better, you're doing exactly what you're supposed to be doing.

A lot of people who make those comments hold on to the old version of you because they are resisting change in their life. They want you to continue to be the person they can remain in sameness with. Your change will begin to make them uncomfortable, and if they are resisting change, your friendship will change. It's inevitable. As you grow and shed old things, unfortunately, some people will get left behind. That's not always a bad thing, nor is it easy, but at times necessary. You don't want to intentionally leave people behind, but not everyone can accompany you to the new season of your life in the same way they once had access to you. Don't feel bad for your evolution.

Change and growth are necessary in life. If you're not growing, you're basically dying. Who wants to die before they've reached their full potential? Not I, and neither should you. I've heard people say they want to die empty. Meaning they left nothing on the table. Everything they were sent to this earth to accomplish, they did. I believe that everyone was sent here with their own mission. Even if you have a similar mission as someone else, you'll go about it differently because they are them, and you are you. You're not going to deliver it the same or put the same spin on it. No one should aspire to be the same. Put your blinders on and be the best you that you can be. No one else can do it but you. You're probably thinking, Shanice girl, what does this have to do with my Marriage? Everything!

I'm here to tell you that if you think being a married woman hasn't changed you, I'm willing to bet that you're wrong. And in the event that you are right, I challenge you to dive deep and figure out what you're holding on to that's keeping you where you were. The girl you were as a single woman was not meant to carry the cargo of the woman you are today. Let that sink in. My husband often says, *"that's just who I am,"* that's not an excuse not to work on yourself. If both parties in the Marriage clung to that's just who I am, how amenable would either of you be to growing for the betterment of your relationship? Growth is necessary for the road you're traveling, and if you're growing, you're changing. Embrace it! Imagine a miner digging through the soil for gold. You are the miner of your own life. We don't want to forget the girl who made us the woman we are today. We want to dig through our soil and figure out, *"Hey, this is good, this is my gold."* There will be good things that you will hold onto, like the loyalty you've always had. However, that procrastinator has to go. It was okay to live with 5 years ago, but you can't take it into this season. Pray about who you desire to be and let God prune your leaves. He'll leave the fruit and dispose of the weeds if you let him (don't cling to those dead ends!).

Just as the Mrs. you once were had needs and desires, so does the now Mrs. Get to know those desires. Many times people, especially women, walk into marriage with these undiscussed expectations. We hold expectations not only for our husbands, but also for ourselves. If we're honest, many of us had envisioned ourselves as a wife before we actually became one. If you have expectations of your husband, tell him! He's not physic. If you have needs that are needed to be met by your husband and he's falling short in that area, let him in on that secret! You may find yourself annoyed/irritated by small things (maybe you don't even know it's a desire of yours because you haven't taken the time to self-evaluate what's important to you). Discuss that with your husband! The common denominator here is communication (which we're going to dive all the way into).

What are you expecting of yourself that is unrealistic or requires more from you than you have to give? Did you imagine that you'd be cooking a hot meal 6 days a week? Maybe you even started that way, but now you have small children who require a lot of time and cooking 6 days a week isn't working. Instead of frustrating yourself trying to meet this self-imposed obligation, figure out what really works. If it's cooking 3 times a week, eating some leftovers, and then delivering twice a week, figure it out. Often in Marriage, we carry around this guilt of falling short in our roles, but who are we falling short to? If we're falling short against our measurement, we need to check in with ourselves and shift some things. We aren't doing anything but frustrating ourselves by holding on to some sort of standard set years ago that we can no longer meet.

Something else to remember when it comes to expectations is, any unsaid expectation is an unrealistic expectation of your husband. Again, he is no mind reader. We can't hold them accountable to some standard that we've never made clear. I know I hold myself to specific internal standards that I don't communicate, and then, without even realizing it, I hold my husband to those same standards. Writing it out, I'm shaking my head at myself. Not only am I putting these standards on myself that no one else asked of me, but then I'm taking my crazy a step further by expecting my husband to fall in line with those same standards.

How sway? If you're anything like me, I write this to say you are not alone, but also we've got to do better. First and foremost, we need to unpack why we're putting some of these expectations on ourselves. Are they a part of our core values? Do they add to our happiness? If so, then great, it's okay to keep them for yourself, as long as you aren't causing more harm than danger by holding yourself accountable to these things. After you decide that for yourself, figure out if these expectations you're unknowingly putting on your husband are in line with what you both decided would be key for your Marriage. For example, if the standard you're holding yourself to is not past 2 am, you want to ensure that you're always home before that time. Your reasoning for that may be, I don't want to be out with people who may have been drinking and on the road. I want to make sure I get a certain amount of sleep, and I want to be respectful of my husband. Now say you're holding your husband to that same standard but haven't said it out loud to him.

Assess why you would like him to follow that standard. Then you want to make sure that you're not imposing something on him that you both haven't deemed as necessary. If you feel strongly enough about the standard, then you should discuss it. Notice I said discussion, not tell him what the standard is. No one wants to be told what to do all the time by anyone. By communicating this standard with your husband, you can let him know why it's important to you. He can let you know why it may or may not be doable for him, and then you two can come up with a compromise that fits your Marriage.

Remember, you should NOT be setting any standards or expectations in your household based on someone else's.

Marriage is not one size fits all, and your Marriage should be custom fit to you and your husband. The minute you begin to communicate what you need and desire, you can eliminate the internal struggle you have when your husband is doing something you don't want him doing that you never told him, lol. See how crazy that looks?! We're driving ourselves insane over something(s) we never made clear and our husbands have no clue about. Give him the opportunity to be in the know of what is expected and also to let you know whether or not that may work for him and you two as a couple.

Communication, communication, communication! If you've been in any kind of relationship for any amount of time, you've heard this word used and used some more. If you're married and searching for some mystical sure-fire way to have a great marriage, I'm sure you've heard that communication is vital. I'm not arguing that point, but I'm adding a layer. Self-reflect! Before you start flying off the handle and getting frustrated, sit down and figure yourself out. You're not the same woman you were. Figure out who you are now. What is serving you in this season of life?

You have new desires, needs, and requirements. Figure out what it is that you want, not what other people want for you. Don't lose yourself in the vow that you made to your spouse. You will both be at your best for each other when you're fulfilled individually. It's probably a good time to dig into you and stand firm in what you need and require from both of you. If you don't have a clear vision of who you are or who you want to be, it's that much easier for you to get swept up in the Marriage. How can you champion someone you don't really know? When you know what's important to you, you can have meaningful conversations with your spouse not only about what you need but what you can give (it's not a one-way street ever). Having these conversations is vital in a healthy Marriage.

It will also keep you from having contradictory requests, which can become confusing and frustrating for your husband to try to keep up with. Be sure and then clear in what you need. Imagine your husband being closed off, lashing out, and being short-tempered, and you not knowing why. You'd probably be frustrated, annoyed, and finding ways to avoid him. Now imagine him sitting you down and saying, at this point in his life, he does not feel as fulfilled in his career (something that has nothing to do with who you are personally), and he is thinking about going back to school to change the trajectory of his career. He would appreciate your support in his return to school, and once he's finished with that goal, he'll be better able to assist you with home life.

Now which option sounds more desirable for you? He communicated to you that his funk has nothing to do with you, or he told you where his source of frustration is coming from and has asked you to support him in advance of taking any action. Now flip it. This is how we should strive to relay messages to our spouses. Not after we've been a complete monster for months, even if it's a difficult conversation to have, it's easier than bottling it up and your resentment seeping out through your actions. When you're married to someone and in the same spaces more often than not, you're not hiding anything by keeping quiet. You may not verbally say anything, but your physical communication will begin to leak your story. I feel like we women get a bad rap as being moody. Now, don't get me wrong, I can be president of the moody club, but when I think about it, my actions are usually off because there is something I'm not verbally saying. I'm suppressing thoughts and emotions that are trickling out in my actions. Usually, once I let the air out of my balloon by communicating, I feel a whole lot better!

There are two things I know to be true. First, God put you and has kept you here for a reason beyond being someone's wife or mother. Second, God loves Marriage. I do not believe that God would have us shrink in who we are as individuals because of being married women. There is purpose tied to Your Marriage, and there is also purpose in who you are on your own.

Don't abandon who you are because of the blessing of Marriage. I want you to commit to love yourself and pray for yourself for a week. Once you master the week, move on to two weeks. Keep going until loving & praying for yourself is something that comes naturally to you. Make a prayer list where the prayers listed are only for you. What are your current worries, fears, hopes & dreams? How can you begin to get closer to the woman you want to be? It starts with you, sis!

Reflection

1. In a few words, what does Marriage mean to you?

_____

_____

_____

_____

_____

_____

_____

2. Close your eyes and envision your *"dream"* marriage. Write down what you saw in that vision.

_____

_____

_____

_____

_____

_____

_____

3. Are you living out the Marriage that you desire currently? If not, what small changes could lead to you having the Marriage you desire? If yes, what could take you from good to great? If you aren't married, what would a fulfilling marriage look like to you?

_____

_____

_____

_____

_____

_____

4. When is the last time you felt like you didn't want the night to end with your spouse? What were you doing? What would it take to make that activity a constant in your lives?

_____

_____

_____

_____

_____

_____

5. Do you and your husband have standing check-ins? If not, start by scheduling them monthly. If that works, maybe move to bi-weekly. Try setting an agenda to stay on task (it doesn't have to be a formal meeting, but it will keep you on task). These meetings can set the stage to discuss your personal goals and what you may need from him to assist. If you already have them, are they something you both look forward to? Challenge here: find a way to make them fun!

_____

_____

_____

_____

_____

_____

_____

_____

_____

_____

_____

6. Do you have a goal number for date nights? If not, set a goal that's doable for your Marriage and stick to it! If you already have a goal number for date nights, I'm challenging you to step it up! Increase that number.

_____

_____

_____

_____

_____

_____

_____

_____

_____

_____

_____

Giving Him The Best

THAT YOU'VE GOT!

Have you ever had a waitress at a restaurant go above and beyond to make sure you had a fantastic experience? How did that make you feel? Besides wanting to leave a perfect tip, I'm sure it added to your pleasant experience and made you want to return the kindness for even more kindness. Those kinds of interactions are contagious! If someone is going out of their way to ensure you're taken care of and happy, it's hard to meet that kindness with wrath. The same way kindness works in interactions with strangers, and it works with your husband also. Giving good love is usually reciprocal.

When someone pays you a compliment, it's almost a natural response to say thank you and repay the favor. Same with love, if someone loves you well, it's hard to turn around and be nasty to them. Often, especially if you were single for a while before Marriage, it's natural to look out for your best interest. You know to say I want and I need, and I require often. It's easy to ask yourself if your husband is checking off all your boxes and loving you well, but when was the last time you asked yourself if you were loving your husband well? And not just giving him what you have leftover from all of your other responsibilities, but putting significant effort into expressing love for your husband. We're quick to say love is an action, but are we acting it out in our marriages? Are we putting in the action behind our *"I love you"*?

Sometimes we can get so caught up in what's important to us and what he is doing for us that we don't stop to assess ourselves. Marriage is not one-sided. We are joined in matrimony to serve one another. If each person in the Marriage is concerned about the other's well-being and what they need, then guess what? All bases are covered. Everyone is being loved well. In Marriage, it is not your primary job to monitor your own love tank. It is your job to monitor your husband's tank, and if it's looking empty, you want to have the gas on hand to fill it and vice versa. Don't be so worried about the where, what, when, and why of your own love tank that you forget that your husband even has a tank.

Once you communicate your love language and what you desire to your husband, leave the weeds of how he fills that tank to him. You work on the details of how you're filling his tank because sometimes we can forget he even has a tank, lol. Show your husband good, authentic, unwavering love as often as you can. You will benefit without even realizing it (not that you should be doing things in Marriage just for the benefit, but it does pay off). When it comes to loving your husband well, it takes a little more effort when you're in each other's presence daily because by human nature, things that we see all the time lose the new and shiny effect after a while. After the honeymoon phase, we have to look for that new and shininess purposefully. We can do that by intentionally exploring new and fun things together and creating opportunities for new shared experiences.

Exploring new things together bonds us and gives us something to look forward to as a unit. It also gives us new things to talk about because when you're around each other all the time, it's common for conversations to get stale. It is a given that the new and shininess of Marriage will fade, but there are ways to counteract that. When the newness fades, you have to be intentional in finding the goodness in your Marriage. I'm not saying it's easy, and there is goodness every waking moment of every day. I will say you get what you look for. If what you're trying to find is goodness, I'm sure it's there to be discovered. If it's not there, I challenge you to create it. It takes effort, but it's worth it. If it were easy, every married person would be living the Marriage of their dreams, but this is a part of the work.

Most times, people who are not yet married will ask, what is the work that married people talk about? It's kind of hard to explain because it's in the little everyday things. You know when you'd rather go to bed than stay up and have a date night in, Lol. Everyone has heard someone say, Marriage is work! That's because it is. We have to decide that we're going to do the things we don't want to do when we don't feel like doing them for the good of our Marriage.

The golden rule we learned as kids is still the golden rule in Marriage.

Treat others as you want to be treated. The thing is, you may feel like you aren't being treated the way you want to be treated. I get it, I'm a recovering tit for tat addict. But who wins in that space? It might feel good at the moment, but in the long-term, how fun is that? If you're going to be seeing each other and raising each other on something, let it be on something good. Cue, Anita Baker, give that man the best you've got, and I'm sure you won't be disappointed. Sometimes people need to be reminded how to treat others. There is no better teacher than being an example.

I've seen repeatedly that you can't change a person, but you can influence them. Be the best influence you can be to your husband. After a while, even if he isn't verbal about it, he'll begin to pick up some of your behaviors. It may be as simple as you wanting him to read more, so instead of watching TV before bed, you begin going to bed with a book. Don't say anything (have you noticed the more you nag on something, he lags on it). Just make reading a part of your daily routine. And see if you don't notice him taking a new interest in reading more.

It's hard to be close to a fire and not get warm. As you're acting like the bigger person, you're modeling the behavior you want to see. Not only are you influencing him for the better, but more often than not, you're becoming a better version of yourself in the process. In today's world, many people want to be an influencer to strangers, but sometimes our best influence is right under our roof. As you're influencing your husband, begin praying for him. What are some things that you would like to see him change from? Maybe something you'd like to see him add. The book example could be one, or it could be working out and eating healthier.

> The Bible tells us it's better to live in a corner on
> the roof of a house than with a nagging wife.
> I lie to you not, look it up for yourself
> **Proverbs 25:24**

No one wants to hear someone lecturing or nagging them all the time. It takes away from the peace of the home. But I've never heard someone say, please don't pray for me. Turn the complaints about your husband to God for the betterment of him. First of all, you want to make sure this change you want to see is not just a selfish request and that it`s really for his well-being. Ask God for His will to be done in your husband's life. Be steadfast in your prayers and be sensitive to the work that you may have to put in. If you're praying for your husband to improve his diet and you're the one who goes grocery shopping, you have a part in that. Stop buying the Coke and cookies and then asking him to do better.

The harsh truth is, sometimes it's us (ouch), and God will have to start with us first. Also, ask yourself the requests that you have for your husband, are you willing to be who you are asking him to be? You want him to read more? Are you willing to put down the trash tv and do some reading? You want him to become healthier, are you willing to forgo the dessert and workout 3 times a week? We can't possibly think that God is going just to grant our requests like a genie and leave us in our mess. We have to be ready and willing to accept our part in what the change will look like.

As I write this book, I've been given a real-life example (that's just how God works). Storytime! My husband came to me and let me know he wanted to take a guy's trip. Now I can't be the only wife who dislikes when their husband is out of town. I've always disliked him for leaving me, but this time (after some spirited fellowship, lol). I went to the Lord in prayer. I wish I could say I prayed an upstanding prayer, but the truth is I prayed to God to stop this trip. I don't want him to go. Help me, do something, God! After that prayer, I sealed it and considered it done.

Y'all, I lie to you not. In a few days, God had softened my heart to the trip. I wasn't upset about it anymore. I had clarity about why this trip was important to him and why he needed it. God softened my heart so much and worked in me to the point where I ended up apologizing to my husband for my actions and not understanding at first. I didn't even realize this had happened until I was retelling the story to my therapist. I had to laugh. God! That wasn't my prayer, and I wanted you to do something about the trip (lol)! This is exactly how it happens many times.

We go to God to fix what we perceive to be the issue, and the answer to the prayers is fixing us. Working on our heart and mindset. I probably have 100 more examples just like this, but God dropped this situation right down in the middle of me writing this, so I had to share. And if I can just dig into the main issue for a second. I had to work with my therapist about why I had such a disdain for him leaving me for a few days. I had to work that stuff out in me. My husband should not be bound to me because I'm demanding him to stay with me at all times.

First, that's not fair, and secondly, it's not genuine. When he is with me, I want it to be, because he wants to be. I can't be the best wife I can be to him until I work out some deep underlying issues I have in me. There are things that I didn't even know I was dealing with until I decided to go ahead and start therapy. My father was never around growing up, and I never really looked at myself as having daddy issues because my mom did a great job, and I had my grandfather around as a father figure since birth. However, I've been masking (well, not really, lol) or dealing with abandonment issues.

At no fault of his own, my husband had to take the brunt of my mess caused by my father's absence. That's not his fault, and honestly, he's done more than enough to prove to me that he is nothing like my father. It is up to me to clean out the mess of my childhood closet so that those issues don't continue to plague my Marriage. In order to give him the best that I've got and ask for the same in return, I have to do some work! The theme here, to give him the best that we've got, we've got to work on us!

Have you ever sat in a room of other seasoned wives (not just seasoned in age, but married for a while, lol). They'll tell you there is no secret to a happy marriage (and there isn't), but there is a piece of advice that stands the test of time. Ready for it? Work on being the best version of yourself. Many of us think that we're supposed to be the best example to people outside of our home, and yes, we should strive to be a good example to other women and Christians, but our biggest stage is at home. We get the best return on investment at home. Do you want 'just because of gifts?'Come home with a just because gift. Do you want to have prayer time together? Begin by grabbing his hand and praying out loud for the both of you.

These are small examples of things where you can begin to lead and then watch him step up to the plate. There is no secret sauce to Marriage. We have to be willing to be vulnerable with what we desire and need and then be willing to be that for him. How can we request what we are not willing to give? There is also a perfect way to figure out what your husband stands in need of without just prying. When was the last time you asked him how you could pray with him? That offers you an opportunity to know what he's currently dealing with and show support and love for him by standing with him or in the gap for him in prayer. Your husband wants to know that you're on his team and not just worried about looking good as a team but genuinely playing as a team. You're only as strong as your weakest link. It's in our best interest to go to the battlefield of prayer with and for our husbands (but also be ready to have your mess pointed out and sometimes corrected, lol). We have to do some work to reap the harvest. We can't look at our neighbor's grass if we've never watered our own lawn. Of course, theirs looks greener if it's being taken care of (but it could also just be turf, just saying)!

If you all have never taken the **5 Love Languages Test**, take it tonight (that is your homework from this chapter). It's such a good way to know how to sometimes verbally and nonverbally communicate with your husband so that they receive it. It is our tendency as humans to love others in the way we would want to be loved, but just because that's how we want to be loved doesn't mean that is how they receive it. Not only do you get to find out how your husband best receives love, but he will find out the same about you without you having to complain about him never bringing you home flowers or just because gifts.

He'll know that if acts of service are your love language, then cleaning the kitchen is a great way to show his appreciation for you. And it takes some time to get it down, it's not like you take the test, and then immediately you begin loving him just right. It just plants the seed, and it's always something to fall back on. If his love language is words of affirmation and you realize it's been a long time since you've paid him a compliment, find something good to let him in on. I recommend taking this test annually. Both of you are changing, and the older you get, the things you appreciate the most may change. The thing about Marriage is, if both parties strive to make the other happy, everyone is covered on the happiness train.

I was raised by a strong single mom, so at the back of my mind, I'm always trying to live up to this crazy thought that I have to be able to take care of myself. Now while it is smart to know how to do things for and by yourself, it shouldn't be a daily thought and something you're working towards (unless you're working towards divorce, which in that case you've picked up the wrong book). Yes, know how to care for yourself, but don't hold back from your husband and then, in turn, in your Marriage.

I'm going to let you in on another secret, the key to receiving vulnerability from your spouse is first to be vulnerable. You have to be open and willing to be raw with your spouse. Show him a side of yourself that is reserved just for him and no one else. What is the use in holding back in Your Marriage? Does it benefit no one? What are you holding in your back pocket? Even if, God forbid, it doesn't work out, you can go forward knowing you gave it all you could. You gave it your whole self, and there is no shame in that. I know I found myself holding back sometimes because I felt like I had to present myself as strong and capable of being by myself. I felt the need to *"protect"* myself from the man I decided to become one with. But why? Is the goal to be by myself? If not, I'm doing myself a disservice.

Men want to feel needed. And sometimes, our need to feel like independent women is counteractive to the need of our husbands. I'm pretty sure they are confident in your abilities as a woman. Showing that you're strong and independent inside of your home isn't really beneficial. Put all your cards on the table and let him love you fully! My therapist asked me recently, a worst-case scenario, that what if your husband decided not to come home. My immediate reaction was to say I'd be fine. She looked at me like girl?! Would you? You've been with this man for about half of your life. Holding on to my *"strong woman act,"* I responded yes, I'd be okay eventually. She continued by asking how?

So I had to think. Girl, you would not be fine!! You'd be devastated! Life as you know it would change forever, and it's okay to say that you would not just bounce back like a robot if that changed. Who am I fronting for? Why is it my instant response to say, I'd be good?! Issa LIE! Now let's look at that a little deeper. If I'm lying to myself like that, the odds are that I'm putting that same energy out to my husband. I'm good, I can do this without you. Which, at first glance, doesn't seem that bad, right? But look at it a little closer. Essentially I'm giving off the vibe that you aren't valuable, and I don't really need you. That's not the reality. Who is winning if I walk around like, that is the truth when it isn't? Not only am I tricking myself and holding back on my true feelings, but at the same time, I'm minimizing my husband's role and value in my life, not just to me but to him as well. I don't know about y'all, but I want to feel like I bring value to my husband and that if God forbid I vanished tomorrow, he would feel it.

So why would I be walking around this house acting as if he is disposable?! As black a woman (I can only speak from the black woman's experience), we have to let go of the struggles of our mothers and grandmothers. I'm walking around here carrying a burden that isn't mine to carry. My man has proven to be a rock for me. He's proven that he loves and cares for me time and time again. He shows up for me, and I love and appreciate him for that. My actions should reflect that. I have to let go of the strong black woman torch and put on my soft, lovable wife torch if I want to see my Marriage grow into all that it's supposed to be (and I feel that for more than just myself).

Everyone wants to feel valued. Apart from showing that value is respect, and I know you've heard time and time again, respect for men is like love for a woman. Your husband is your husband. Not your mom's husband, your best friend's husband, not the ex-boyfriend who played with your time and broke your heart. He shouldn't have to pay for the mistakes of any of those men (insert Musiq Soul Child's previous cats, lol). Clear your plate sis, and make room for the good man God has given you! Give him all of you. You both deserve it!

If you want your Marriage not just to survive but also to thrive, you have to give it the best you've got. All that you've got, and you can't do that by holding back 25% of yourself for yourself. Trust that God has blessed you with your husband, and even if he isn't the best husband today, he's working on it. You win nothing by holding back yourself. Give it 1000% every day. If we strive for 1000%, hopefully, we'll land somewhere around 98, lol. Life itself is difficult.

Add in the element of being the caretaker of someone's heart. It's a huge task, but it doesn't have to be as hard as we tend to make it. I know a lot of us to think, well, when he gives 100%, I'll give 100%, but the truth is some days he won't have it to give 100%, and so you'll pick up where he can't and vice versa. When you don't have your 100% to give, he'll step in and provide what it is you stand in need of. The goal is to be the best home **team** you could possibly be, and that means giving it your all even when you don't feel like it.

Words From A Wise Wife

"Sometimes in Marriage, it takes more than meeting your spouse halfway. Sometimes, you're required to meet your spouse exactly where they are and work your way towards middle ground together."

-Rhea Plummer
Creator of Fab Wives
Married 12 years

Reflection

1. Clear your schedules, and YOU plan a date night. Be creative, it doesn't have to be expensive or even out of the house. But it's on you to show up and show out!

_____

_____

_____

_____

_____

_____

_____

_____

_____

_____

_____

_____

_____

_____

2. Plan a _____(insert your last name) Team Meeting. Create an agenda where you will go over the goals and desires you both have for this upcoming year. Maybe come up with a chant or a mantra for this year.

_____

_____

_____

_____

_____

_____

_____

3. Eat dinner together 3 times this week with no electronic devices. If this is something you are already doing, see if you can add a coffee/tea date to your morning routine twice this week.

_____

_____

_____

_____

_____

_____

_____

4. If you could only ask God for one thing for your Marriage (it doesn't have to be something you don't currently have or do), what would it be? Write it down and commit to praying for it for a month and watch God work.

_____

_____

_____

_____

_____

_____

_____

5. Make a list of the top 5 things you value most in your Marriage. Share that list with your husband and ask him to share his top 5. Commit them to memory and make them a priority.

_____

_____

_____

_____

_____

_____

_____

6. In what ways could you change for the better in your Marriage? What actionable steps could you take to get you there? If you aren't married yet, how can you begin being the wife you want to be now, before actually being a wife?

_____

_____

_____

_____

_____

_____

_____

_____

_____

_____

_____

_____

_____

There's No 'I

IN TEAM

A Long time ago, I learned a short poem that rung true for the experience I was in, but this poem also reigns true in Marriage.

> *"I, me, my, mine, these are things that do not rhyme.*
> *Us, we, our, together, these are things that last forever."*

Cheesy, I know, but easy to remember and true? Yes, while you are very important, and I pray that you are tending to your needs first because what will come out of that overflow will benefit everyone connected to you. This mentality when it comes down to your Marriage is detrimental to the success of your marriage. When you take a step back and look at the whole big picture of your Team, AKA your Marriage, there are not two sides *"fighting"* to win their way.

You want to see a holistic view of what works well for the whole pie, not the individual slices. We're human, and many of us were single for a longer time than we've been married, which means sometimes we will default to the 'I know best ideology.' What would be helpful to the Marriage would be to play to each other's strengths and always come together to make the best decision for the team. We don't want to approach tough or important decisions like we're going into the court of law, and it's the defense against the prosecution, and we have a judge to convince that our side is right.

We want to have an open mind that maybe, just maybe, our husband has some great value to add to the situation, and we want him to believe the same about us. Marriage will force an amount of compromise out of you that you didn't even know you had inside. The compromise that marriage requires of us isn't the *"fine you're right kind"* either, lol. It's the actual coming together and being open and agreeable to whatever the right decision is for your marriage as a unit-not begrudgingly agreeing to go along with your husband's plan and waiting for it to fail.

Ask me how I know about that? Lol. We have to trust that sometimes his answers are the right ones for the situation, and sometimes ours will be correct. Other times it will be the blend of both answers to make the ultimate best decision for us at that time. Going in with an open mind towards trusting our husbands' thoughts and actions is key to trusting him to be a significant contributor to how we will live our lives. Do you trust the man that God gave you to make good decisions? And it will take time to get there effortlessly, but once you do, I think you'll agree that it's not as bad as it sounds. As women who sometimes have to make decisions in other areas of our lives all day, it feels good to come home to a soft place and know you don't have to shoulder all responsibility there and be the key decision-maker as well. Just as you pick your battles with arguments, we should pick our battles with decisions.

I know early in marriage, I would find myself holding on to my opinions and thoughts just because I didn't want to be wrong or *"concede"* in the argument. That's not serving me or my marriage because if my husband has a better idea and I know it's the better idea, what am I trying to prove by holding on to my not-so-great idea? We often talk about men and their egos, but ladies, sometimes our egos come out swinging as well.

We want to hold on to ideas and opinions just because. Who is winning when we do that? It isn't our husband or us. Until we realize there is no individual winner, but when the Marriage wins, we both win, then we can change our frame of mind and see a shift in the way we approach our decision-making as a team.

Words From A Wise Wife

"Keep it simple, and always remember you're playing for the same team!"

-Charisse Weiss
Owner of Red Lips Red Wine
Married 10 years

Husband Before...

KIDS/FRIENDS/NUCLEAR FAMILY

Okay, you're a wife. Now what? How do you fully step into that role? We've gone over how we show up for ourselves and how we should show up for the betterment of our marriages, but now let's talk about priorities. We women hold so many roles that are important to us. Sisters, daughters, mothers, entrepreneurs, employees, and the list goes on. It's hard to balance all the hats we wear and for this reason, we have to understand that we can't. We cannot balance everything. Somewhere once upon a time, some woman thought she could balance all things well. Other people thought she was balancing all things well. And so somehow, women everywhere thought that was the goal.

The thing is that's not possible, lol. If you want to become an expert at one thing, you have to put more time into studying and becoming an expert at it. If you're trying to become an expert at all the things, you'll be an expert at nothing because you cannot do all the things well. You have to choose. I know, we live in a world today where we want all the things, we want to do all the things and think we should be able to. Now, in reality, yes, you can do all the things, and in that, some things are just going to be piss pore because there is only one you. If you want to do something at a high calibre, you have to give it more of yourself than you give to things that are just not as important. Like right now, writing this book is important to me. I also made a goal at the beginning of the year to read one book a month. Both of those things are important to me in this season. However, I have prioritized writing this book, so if I don't finish reading a book in this month of writing, that's okay. Some things are not going to get the same attention as others annnnnd you guessed it, that's okay. If we are stretching ourselves thin to try and give our best to all the different roles we play, all the areas will suffer.

I'm stressing this point because our husbands will notice when they are lower than they should be (or want to be) on the priority list. Unfortunately, many of them won't say anything. They'll continue to let you spread yourself thin until there is a major issue or argument, and then it will come up. We'll be *"blindsided"* because they haven't said anything, and we thought they didn't notice (jokes on us, lol). We want to get ahead of that moving train by making sure he's at the top of the list and knows it. Sidebar if we think we're putting him at the top of the list and he doesn't feel it, then he's probably not at the top of the list, and we need to do some digging and reorganizing. A shift needs to occur as we fully step into the role of wife.

To be an excellent example in our marriages, we have to be giving our Marriage and husband the time and effort they need to flourish. There is a saying that where you spend most of your time is your priority.

The Bible says,
"Where your treasure is, there your heart will also be."
Matthew 6:21

For a planner like me, open up your monthly spread, and what you see most often is your top priority. (Remember that I told you earlier to add yourself to your schedule as well). Many of us are guilty of prioritizing the wrong things without even noticing it. We think we have to be on call for all of our friends because that's what good friends do. We have to do the extra project at work because that's how we get ahead. We have to stay up late cleaning the kitchen because that's the only time we can get it done (hey, go hire the cleaning company, lol), but I digress. As we're doing all of these, we think our husbands understand that we are needed in all these other areas. But do they?

Let me let you in on something; if he's feeling under appreciated and unrecognized, he doesn't care about what friend or project needs you because he needs you more. Now, trust me when I say I feel your internal stretch, lol. We know our husbands should be a top priority but are our actions backing that up? Are we living out what we say and know to be true? We're so busy living our lives that we don't realize what we think and what is actually happening might be two different things. If we say we prioritize dinner together as a family, but four times a week, we allow work to keep us beyond our committed time, therefore missing dinner with our family, work is the priority as shown by our actions. We have to put our actions where our mouth is. We also don't want only lip service to our husbands. We want them to know that we mean it, and it's going to get done if we say something. We don't want them to begin to not take our word at face value because of our actions or lack thereof. Prioritize making the main thing what it should be and not just talking about it.

Before getting married, we belonged to our nuclear family, who we've been with our whole lives. The nuclear family is your mom, dad, sisters, brothers, or sometimes grandparents that raised us. I heard it said that our nuclear family is our university for life. Our formative years were spent with our nuclear family, and there are things that we still think and do now because of our roots in that nuclear family. Our family has made us who we are (for better or worse), and sometimes it's hard to *"leave and cleave"* to our new family.

Leaving and cleaving are necessary to create your family values and norms. It's also exciting to create your version of family. We cherish the relationships in that family (as we should), they know us better than anyone else sometimes, and they provide comfort and familiarity. They understand certain things with no explanation; they just get us! But once we get married, there is a shift that must take place.

It's hard and may take practice and unlearning certain dependent behaviors. I have an amazing relationship with my mother. She was my best friend growing up, hands down (she was still a momma, don't get it twisted, lol). I knew she had my back. I knew she loved me unconditionally and provided me comfort like no other human. Until I was a married woman, she was the top priority in my life.

I remember on my wedding day us dancing together and her crying (my mother does not cry easily or often). I was so confused and told her confidently nothing would change. Again, I was hours into being married; I had no idea what was on the other side of 'I do.' I now understand that my mother, a married woman, and a mother, knew that things couldn't be the same with the new role I was taking on. I was moving in and starting a life with my husband, and that had to take precedence. That would now shift positions with her, and that is a hard pill to swallow (some of us still haven't swallowed that pill, priorities! ladies, priorities!!).

My boys are young, and I know when they grow up, I have to shift positions. It will be difficult for me, but this is the circle of life and, subsequently, the sequence of events. Now I'm not saying your mom, dad, sisters, and/or brothers are no longer important; however, you go to sleep and wake up in a different household. One that you set the tone for every single day. If you want peace in your home, your home has to come first. Your current household is a priority in your life, and that's just what it is. We can't effectively manage two households. I do understand as parents age and outlying issues arise, you have to help where you can.

The key here is where you can. Before you begin volunteering time and effort, check in with your spouse and see what is needed there first. Because your husband loves you, I'm sure he will support whatever role you need to take on the time. It's just important to make him feel included in a decision that will affect his household. As a wife, it is so important to me to be the heart of my home. If I'm over-concerned with what's going on in a household outside of mine, how can I provide that warm, soft place for my home? You can try, but it will conflict with what you're trying to do.

It goes back to communication and planning. If you know you're needed elsewhere for a few nights a week, maybe plan ahead with your husband about scheduling and what you can and cannot handle, and where you'll need to tag Team. Don't just go ghost (this is a marriage, not insecure (the HBO series follow me here, lol). Communicate where your energy may be divided and how you plan to make sure you don't slack at home.

Maybe it isn't your nuclear home that is competing for your attention. Perhaps you have a career that you LOVE, and not only do you love it, but it also provides a great life for you and your family, so you give it a lot of your time and attention. One word boundaries! Ahhhhh, that retched 'B' word. I can't just throw out the word boundaries and act like I have it all together in that area. I do not. Setting boundaries and working through them is something I'm battling with. I sometimes tend to be a people pleaser, and if I'm honest, battle with FOMO (fear of missing out).

I know some of y'all feel me on this (don't leave me hanging, lol). These things cause me to lack boundaries, but I ignore them even if I have some set. A fun girl's night comes calling, but I said I needed to be in bed by 9 o.clock to be productive in the morning. Who needs productive mornings anyway?! I go to the girl's night, which was fun, but then I pay for it by beating myself up in the morning when I sleep in and miss my morning routine, which has now derailed the whole day I had planned because of my lack of boundary keeping.

….read this slowly.

We all need boundaries, or we'll go crazy. When we lack boundaries, the person who suffers the most is We! When we suffer, it bleeds into other areas of our life, and now everything is being affected by our inability to set up and keep important limits around our priorities. Set up the boundaries, Sis! Boundary tip in this year of 2021, our smartphones are running our lives. Set up boundaries around when you are going to allow that little thing to take hold of you. I have an iPhone, and I have time limits set on it. This has been a game-changer! I have time limits set on certain apps that drain my time, and then I also have a time set for when I need to be off my phone period. The phone gives me a warning and lets me know, hey! Girl, you have 5 minutes until your limit is up. It's hard to get used to it at first, but it is so necessary. Be in the present, put the phone down. Set up the hard boundaries so that you can live a more intentional, fulfilled life.

Not only is it hard to set the boundaries, but then you have to communicate them (ouch) and stick to them (argh). It's not easy, and it takes practice, but it is necessary to make sure the important things to you get done first. Remember, put on YOUR face mask first before helping anyone else, or you're both as good as dead (harsh, I know, but it's the reality). I just mentioned that we prioritize things in our lives by the amount of time and energy we give them. If something in your life is swallowing up most of your time, no matter how much you might utter something different, that time suck *is* your priority. Even if you love your job, I don't think you want it to come before your husband.

Sometimes we are unaware of the time sucks in our lives. Take inventory! Just pay attention for one week to how much time you're spending on different things in your life. Once you do this self-study, I can almost guarantee there will be pockets of time you're spending somewhere you weren't fully aware of. The great thing is, you can reboot and update your internal software to shift priorities. The choice is ours, it is our life, and how we spend our time is up to us. That audit is important for us to know where the time is going and how we want to reshuffle the time spent on what is important to us. Now momma's, this is a hard one. For those of us who are moms to young children, don't hate me for this. Your husband has to come before the baby(s). I know, I know. I love my children. I thank God for them daily.

However, if we aren't careful about their place in our lives, not only will we suffer greatly, but so will our marriages. I know what you're thinking (well, at least how I felt). They are minor and dependent on me. They won't be this small forever. All of this is true, and I'm not suggesting we neglect our kids. All I'm saying is that our husbands should receive more for the time and attention we give to them. While our babies are young, cute, and cuddly now, they are going to grow up and…leave us (remember the leave and cleave I mentioned earlier? It applies to our kids also). They will become teenagers who have friends and have their lives (shoot, my 5-year-old is already into his friendships, lol).

If we center our lives around our children, we'll be lost and confused when they leave. I've been saying that before we had kids, I didn't want to raise kids together, and then when they leave, we don't know who we're married to. It takes at least 18 years for our children to be completely independent of us, and that's on the low end. If we spend that time consumed with them, there is no way we would be in tune with whom we married. Who do you know that has not changed in 18 years? You will look up, and your husband will be unrecognizable. If the children were a crutch, you wouldn't know how to walk through home life without them when they leave. Our children are brilliant, and they will know when something is off with mommy and daddy. They will know if you're living in a loveless or unfulfilling marriage. We will become dependent on our children for happiness, and they will recognize that if we live that way. I don't know about you, but I'm not trying to be dependent on any teenager (I've been there, haven't I? lol). Yes, we love our kids, but our kids can not be the first on our priority list. They will drive us naught.

As much as I love my boys, I desire adult conversation, date nights, vacations without them. These things continue to make our Marriages strong while we raise our kids. You can do both. They will survive a week without their mommy and daddy (praise God for a village!! lol). Our children have a front-row seat watching us live out what we value. I hope that it will become apparent to them that love and family are important. We also want to be careful that we aren't confiding in our children about their dad (Go back and read that twice). Our children are not our counselors. Even if we aren't purposefully having conversations with our children about their fathers, they listen to the words we say.

Be it out loud ourselves or on the phone with a girlfriend (sidebar… watch any negative talk about your husband to anybody). While our husbands might have great work to do in the role of a husband, they can still be amazing fathers. That is their role to our children, and we shouldn't be tainting the children's views of them with our thoughts and/or words. It's not only inappropriate but can be detrimental to their relationship. They deserve to have a complete and joyous relationship with their dad. If you need to vent about his imperfections as a husband, I would suggest a licensed professional, not his children. Remember when your husband apologizes to you, and you both makeup, you've forgiven him, but your children (and anyone else you've confided in) didn't get the apology and/ or flowers and are still stuck with that negative aftertaste your disagreement left.

A while ago, I was listening to a podcast (shout out to Anatomy of Marriage), and they said the words, *"more is caught than taught,"* which is so true. I repeat this mantra silently to myself all the time. You can say one thing and do another when it comes to your children, but nine times out of ten, they will mimic what they see you doing. The whole 'do what I say, not as I do theory we grew up with, yea no. It doesn't work. My prayer is that my sons will see what a loving marriage looks like, close and personal. I want showing and receiving love to be something they know how to do and display in their adult lives.

They will know they can't play mommy against daddy and vice versa because our team is solid. And a big one that some people with children don't realize is that they'll feel free to go off and live their own lives when the time comes because mommy and daddy are good! You don't want to be responsible for hindering your child's growth because they feel like you need them. We've lived our lives, and our children deserve the same. Please give them the gift of a solid marriage so they don't feel like they can't spread their wings. Our happiness is not the responsibility of anyone else, especially not our kids. I'm definitely not advising you to love your kids any less; simply a charge to say as much as you love your kids, give your husband a little more!

Let's not just stay together because we have kids, but let's work on having the best marriage we can so that our kids reap the dividends. It's okay to get a sitter and make time for just the two of you. It's okay to call in on that village and take a week or so to get lost in the love of your husband. Try to retreat and renew together at least annually, and it doesn't have to be a grandiose trip out of the country every time. The key here is the time spent away from others to recharge as a unit.

As hard as it is to leave my children, when possible, my husband and I go on vacation without them for our anniversary. It is our annual honeymoon. We get to connect, have quiet dinners, dream together, and really get lost in each other uninterrupted. We need it, you need it, and the kids will be okay. You'll be better for it, I promise!

Wise Council

WATCH THE COMPANY YOU KEEP

I know some of us made promises (some unspoken) that we wouldn't let marriage change our friendships or fun-loving side. As I said earlier, change in life, married or not, is inevitable. There is this couple who got married at first sight, and the wife commented that she goes out with her friends from Thursday to Sunday, and she expected that not to change. Ma'am! Would you want to be married to a man who preferred being out every weekend with his friends than to spend quality time with you? We cannot expect to enter into marriage with these kinds of non-negotiable habits and then expect to have the marriage we've always dreamed of.

Again, priorities, boundaries, and making our love an action word will require shifts in other parts of our lives. I love a good girlfriend link up with all things girly (I live with all boys, lol), but the reality is I don't wake up and go to sleep with my friends. My friends and I can disagree for months, and it does not affect how I do my day-to-day activities. I'm not suggesting we throw our friends to the wayside at all. I am saying that they should not and cannot be prioritized over your husband or family, for that matter.

When we had boyfriends, the infamous friendship saying was, I was here before him, and I'll be here after him. The thought behind that was once the relationship falls to pieces, your best girlfriends would be there with pizza and ice cream to help you collect the pieces. That can't be the frame of mind for your marriage. We're in it to win it, and our actions should reflect that. Here we go with another saying, but there will be things your single friends do that you can't do anymore (like staying out all night every weekend) and some that just don't interest you. Your focus has changed, your vocabulary has changed, and your interests have likely changed as well.

Also, keep in mind that just because you have a longtime friend who is like family, you can't share the ins and outs of your new (or not so new) married life with them. Everything in your marriage is not for everybody. Some things are actually only for God. Sometimes your battles have to begin and end spiritually. Friends who have never been married (or maybe they have been married and are divorced) will not understand your viewpoint and therefore cannot advise you on things they know nothing about. Think about you trying to advise a married woman on what they should have done years before you ever entered into marriage. You had no idea what went into it, and there could not possibly give useful counsel. That is okay; say it out loud. Everything is not for everybody.

When you strive for a goal, you have to be careful about who you seek guidance and comfort from. If they haven't obtained the goal you're striving for or at least work towards it themselves (in this instance, the goal is a happy, fulfilling marriage), the likelihood that they're going to advise you in the right direction properly is slim. I wouldn't train for a marathon with someone who never actually completed a marathon themselves. It just doesn't make any logical sense. My husband loves to say if you want to get hot, you have to stay close to the fire.

The fire, in this case, would be people in loving, healthy marriages. Who do you have in arms' reach that you can learn from in the area of marriage? You don't always even have to verbalize to them that you're gleaning from their marriage. You can take mental notes when in their presence, ask clarifying questions or ask for advice in certain areas, and then sometimes, yes, it's completely okay to make it clear that they are your mentor couple. Just like marriage enrichment, a mentor couple can step in and provide some unbiased advice. Sometimes, they've even been through the same situation and share what helped them through that season in their marriage.

The key is identifying that couple together as a couple so that when you turn to the wife on your own, your husband is not offended or surprised. He will know that is a safe place for you as a couple, and you aren't turning to her to gossip but to help you maneuver through whatever issue you might be having individually or collectively. Your mentor couple doesn't necessarily have to be older than you in age, but you definitely don't want them to be in the same season of marriage as you. You would want them to have been married long and have experienced some things so that they can help you maneuver through similar situations.

It would also be good if they are not in close your friend circle (sharing many of the same friends). What you don't want is for you or your husband ever to have wonder if you're in a safe place when seeking counsel in confidentiality. Foster that relationship and watch how that connection positively impacts your marriage. It's crucial to be around what will inspire you to be better. Often, the people who love us most will not be unbiased in their opinions and counsel. I mentioned earlier how close I am with my mother. In many ways, she has been my rock, my entire life. Her opinion and advice to this day are a major part of my decision-making. Because she was the only parent present for me growing up, all my stock was in her.

While my mother has no problem telling me when I may be wrong (lol), it would be difficult if it came down to it to side with someone else over me. When I was dating my husband, I turned to my mom when he was getting on my nerves (and to be honest, she gave me some really good advice, lol). Now that he is my husband, I had to put some boundaries in place with my relationship with my mom when it comes to discussing my husband. As hard as it was to do, it was the right thing to do.

If I go to my mother now and share certain things about my husband or marriage, it's not only my business. I'm sharing my husband's story and issues as well, which isn't always meant for my mother. She's my mother. She will always have my best interest at heart. Whenever you decide to seek wise counsel on your marriage (after consulting with your husband), it should be with someone or a couple whose best interest is the marriage, not you or your husband individually, but the union as a whole. It's hard for the person who grew me inside of her and nurtured me until I was an adult to do that, no fault of her own. I'm sure I would be the same way with my kids. Most people who knew you pre-marriage are going to have your best interest at heart.

This includes your friends. I say all of this to say, and it may be a good idea to throw the whole *"no new friends"* theory to the side and find yourself some cool, like-minded married couples to hang out with. Again, this isn't to say kick all of your single friends from childhood to the side. I'm saying they shouldn't be who you confide in or seek counsel from about your marriage. You should absolutely make time to be amongst your friends, connect with them, let your hair down, and just have a good time.

The good time, however, shouldn't be at the expense of your husband or marriage. Also, just to tiptoe back into priorities for a moment, when you're scheduling your fun girl's nights, make sure you've put just as much effort into planning good times with Bae. Let's say right now you have a standing girl's night every month. You girls get together at a different spot, get cute, laugh, and reminisce on old times, and just have an all-out good time.

You don't miss it, and it's on the calendar in permeant marker (this sounds like a great idea actually now that I think about it, lol). On the flip side of this standing girl's night, you have nothing set in stone with your husband. There is no standing date night, nothing to look forward to on the calendar for the two of you, and you rarely dress up to hang out with him whenever you two might go out. Can you see how this might make him feel? You might be saying, well, we see each other every day, and this is true. But what do you have for the two of you that's standing, not messing with, can't wait to get to its date? If the answer is nothing, your calendar and actions tell your husband that your friendships with your girls are more important than your friendship with him (don't be mad with me, I'm just stating the obvious to the outside world, lol).

The answer to this is not to remove the girl's nights from the calendar. It's to prioritize and put the same kind of effort and energy into date nights with your husband. Maybe you can set it for bi-weekly or monthly. Whatever the frequency, make sure you're setting them. Extra credit tip; get just as cute or cuter to go out with him. Don't beat your face, and put on heels to meet up with the girls, and then throw on sweats and a hoodie to hang out with Bae. He wants that same energy. Hanging around the house, he sees the real you, and I'm sure he loves it. However, remind him of how you caught him on date night ☺.

And while we're talking about friends, let's discuss prioritizing friendship within your marriage. I know the cliché is saying your husband is your best friend, but corny saying aside. Are y'all even friends for real? Like if either of you gets really good news or horrible news, is the first person you want to share it with your spouse? Another reflective question to ask yourself is if you feel like your husband is your best friend, does he feel the same? Take a look in the mirror. Do you give him what he needs from you as his friend? A safe place to be himself, to be silly, to not discuss money or bills, to truly let his actual self show up.

Or can you be overly critical, always serious, never entirely giving him your attention (put the phone down and close the laptop when you sometimes talk, sis)? Does your husband feel fully heard and seen by you? Every human desire deep connection. Even if they don't realize it, we were created for it. We were created to be in connection and communication with other humans. If we are not getting that at home, that can put a significant strain on the relationship.

You have to make space for more than just the *"hallway"* conversations. You know the, *"what's on the schedule, what's for dinner, how was your day small conversations."* This is your person. It would help if you wanted to know the ins and outs of his day, how he's feeling, and some of his deepest desires. You can find out the weather, calendar, and dinner menu by pulling up an app or reading a calendar. What about asking him what went well for you today? What is something you're looking forward to this weekend? What is something you haven't done in a while that you would love to add to the calendar soon? Open the door to fun, thoughtful conversation with your husband. When things become too serious all the time in your relationship, it will no longer feel like an enjoyable, soft place. Lighten it up and often!

When you were dating, I'm sure you cared about the impression you left on your husband, and if you were anything like me, you wanted to convey to him that you had a life outside of him. For me, it was hard to turn that off. I'm not sure if it was something I learned growing up, but as a girlfriend, it was important to me to convey that my world didn't revolve around my boyfriend. I have x,y, z going on; I'll see if I can fit you in. But honey, this is marriage, and we have to reverse that way of thinking and acting. My husband is the priority, and it's important to me that he feels that.

Our actions will speak that loud and clear without us ever saying a word. So we have to ensure our actions are matching our thinking. Our thoughts should be something like I have x,y,z going on, but what does my husband need of me first? See what I did there. I didn't say get rid of x,y,z, keep them (if they're serving you and making you happy in this season of your life). But x,y,z isn't the priority, giving the leftovers to your husband. If you're giving leftovers, be prepared to get the results of a leftover, stale, and cold plate. As the woman, more times than not, we set the tone for our household. We make the house a home, and we should take that role seriously. If it's not feeling too welcoming or soft at home, we're probably missing in action where we should be playing a major role.

We want our homes to be where we love to be; we want it to be a place where our husbands want to be. It should be a sanctuary for both of you. When you look at the word 'sanctuary,' what does that mean to you? Could you write it down? Does it include peace, soft music, laughs, candles, or fresh flowers? It would help if you also got your husband's input on this. Figure out and define what a sanctuary looks and feels like for the both of you, and then execute. Bring it to reality? The home should feel good to both of you! Home is where the heart is if you cultivate that.

A huge part of creating a sanctuary and soft place for our husbands to land is trust. Can he trust you with his feelings, his heart, and his deepest thoughts? I can tell you if your husband thinks that everything he shares with you will end up in a GroupMe chat or a phone conversation with your mom. He is not going to open up to you and be vulnerable. It's like you going to a therapist and there being no confidentiality agreement, and you know once your session is over, your issues will be open for discussion amongst all her friends. Would you open up and share?

If your husband puts up a wall with you, not only will he not be sharing his authentic self with you, but he'll likely have someone else he views as a confidant in his life. We want to be their soft landing place where they feel free to share their heart and honest thoughts. He committed his life and trust to you, not all of your friends and family. Respect his privacy by keeping his private opinions private. A big part of that is knowing what is for the privacy of your marriage and when seeking counsel, seeking wise counsel.

Something that took me some time to get into the habit was, praying to God about handling a situation with my husband. My mother always preached *"pick your battles,"* which basically means everything is not worth the *"fight."* When you feel yourself on the brink of a heated disagreement, AKA an argument, pause and ask yourself, *"Is this worth the argument I'm about to enter?"* Most times, the answer will be no. When you realize that, internally, try your best to deescalate the situation. While everything is not worth a fight, something does deserve a conversation, especially if you don't want to repeat the behavior.

I realized I needed to seek God when I needed to have a conversation with my husband, when I needed to just vent in prayer, or when I really need to seek the wise counsel of a trusted confidant. A lot of people will say, what happens in the household stays in the household. However, while that is true for some things, a mature couple knowing when to seek professional help or turn toward a seasoned trusted couple is key (queue the mentor couple we discussed just a bit ago).

Before marriage, I'm sure you heard married people say marriage is hard, marriage is work, marriage is… Did these married people ever advise on doing the said work and keeping it fresh and fun? Nope! We just entered into it with all the exciting naïve hopes and dreams for our new life together. As a married woman, I'm all about the practical steps we as wives can take to make sure that we're not only living a life that we enjoy but building a marriage we can be proud of. What are some real deal practical steps we can take to help improve our marriage? We know that the work begins with us, right?

So that means making sure that we're whole and happy ourselves, not depending on our husbands to come in and complete us or take us from unhappy to happy. That is work that we have to get done, and if that means that we need to seek professional help from a therapist, that's more than okay. We cannot expect our husbands to be our saviors. They have their trauma and healing to complete. They cannot come into our lives and undo years of issues they didn't create. Don't give them that burden to bear. Self-work aside and attended to, we also need to make sure we're taking time for marriage enrichment.

Marriage enrichment can come in many different forms; Conferences, retreats, books, marriage ministry at church. Anything that you are doing to learn and help you gain tools for success in your marriage is considered marriage enrichment. You both don't have to be reading the same book or listening to the same podcast for it to be marriage enrichment. If you're doing the work and then bringing it back home to introduce it to your husband, it's marriage enrichment. This is essential, a lot of new or married couples think you have to wait until something is wrong to take part in these kinds of activities, but it's quite the opposite.

If you're waiting until something is wrong, you're too late. The good thing about attending a conference or seminar while you're in a good place is, first, it's just more enjoyable for the both of you versus trying to connect when you have a massive boulder in between the two of you. Secondly, you now have those tools and lessons learned for the subsequent misunderstanding or disagreement. You don't want to wait until you're drowning to try to learn how to swim. In the same way, you want to have successful tips and tools under your belt before things start going smooth in your marriage.

Letdowns are a part of human interaction. No one person is perfect, which results in us sometimes letting people down and, you guessed it...being let ourselves down. How we cope with the letdown is vital. It's human and natural to be disappointed when things don't go the way we expected or hoped they would. Allow yourself the time to sit in that for a moment. The keyword is 'a moment.' It's probably best to express why you are let down so you can talk it through with your husband. That way, they can better help you see where things went wrong on their end.

I'm willing to bet that your husband didn't set out to disappoint you; unfortunately, it's the fallout of being an imperfect human. Once you've talked it over (or maybe written it down if you've decided it wasn't worth making a thing out of), allow yourself to let it go. That's right! Let go of whatever it is that had you fuming. Stewing on the letdown will do no good for you, your husband, or your marriage. It happened, it didn't feel good, and you worked through it, now throw it out. It serves no one to think about how things could have gone differently.

"Should've," "could've," "would've," are not helpful in these circumstances. We cannot go back and change what has happened. We can only commit to assessing the situation, communicating clearly what we need, and then moving forward.

I believe everyone needs a HUG in their marriage. This is an acronym that I've come up with to help me be a better wife day in and day out. When you hear it, I want you to think of the actual physical hug. Lead with that; make sure you are actually embracing your husband daily. I know it sounds simple, but if you pay attention, you'd be surprised at how long you can go without actually hugging each other when you're caught up in the day-to-day of life. And no halfway hugs. Stop what you're doing, put down the laundry and hug your husband. Take in his embrace, smell his cologne. Once you make sure you're hugging your husband, ask yourself how I can help my husband. What can I do today to help? Not tomorrow or something next week, but today how can I be of help to him? And that could be through prayer. Ask him aloud, *"babe, how can I help you today"?*

The 'U' stands for uplift. How can you uplift your man today? Even if his primary love language isn't words of affirmation, most men love to hear positive feedback and feel appreciated. This one I don't want you to ask him, but figure out on your own how you can uplift him today. Lastly, let's talk about Grace. That is a huge one. I've talked about how none of us is perfect, and although we know this, somehow, grace toward our spouse still seems to be so difficult. When we constantly hold our husbands to the fire, they might begin to feel like, no matter what they do, it won't be right, so why even attempt to do the right thing? Grace not only works in his favor, but ours also. He's human and imperfect. Give that man some grace!

Perspective is everything. In the moments when I feel like my husband is on the very last nerve ending in my body, I have to remember not to take him for granted. While he may not be perfect, he's mine, and if for some reason he was no longer in my life tomorrow, my life would be drastically different and not in a good way. Just that thought alone is enough for me to forget whatever he's done to get on my nerves and remember he makes my life better, so why harp on the negatives? If I can be very honest with you, this book serves as a diary as I write it.

One of my spiritual mothers and married mentor always tells me that when you're getting ready to do anything in serving other marriages, get ready for yours to be under attack. It sounds scarier than it is, lol. When you're on alert, you're better equipped to handle the issue. I bring this up because, as I write, it may seem like, oh, she has the perfect marriage. FALSE. I'm still learning and relearning many of the lessons I'm writing about. That's the beauty of it, though. I'm working through it real-time, and so it's fresh and not something I think I remember going through. No, these are things that I'm working day in and day out in my own home.

I love my husband, and I have no doubt he loves me, but as we have seen in Hollywood time and time again, love isn't always enough. You have to be intentional about going after the marriage you want. Do the work, improve communication, and indulge in marriage enrichment.

Words From A Wise Wife

"The world is hard enough. Try your best to be a soft space for your husband to land when he comes home."

-Tierra Haynes
Mommy on the Move
Married 11 years

Submission Isn't A

BAD WORD

When the topic of submission comes up to a millennial wife, you might as well have called them out of their name. I have to admit, going into marriage, I thought of submission as an outdated, unnecessary tool that Christian husbands would use to *"control"* their wives. I did not grow up with a submissive mother in the least bit. I don't know if I had any role models in my life growing up that I would call *"submissive."* So I'm not sure where I got the negative connotation from or why it was just looked at as a dirty word, but by living a little and doing my research,

I now see it in a new light. Follow me here a bit if you're anything like what I used to be. I'm sure you were ready to skip over this section with the mention of the word, but it can actually be, whispers a good thing. So we're talking about winning teams, right? Most teams have a coach. The coach is not necessarily a person who is better than anyone on the team. The coach is typically someone who provides direction and prepares the team to go out and win (however they go about it). A good coach will take input from and assessment of the team before they make any calls. The coach could never win a championship on their own without the support of the team. I want you to look at submission as a strategy for your winning team. It does NOT mean that you shrink and do whatever your husband says, Nah! We're not going for that. Have you ever heard of the coach being named the MVP? No, because while they might lead, they are not the totality of the team. The team is made up of players. Your husband is a coach and a player. Things took a significant shift for me when I heard the word submission broken down for marriage.

The word sub in this context means *"under"* (which at first sight is why we wives are like uuuunnh uhhh I'm not under nobody!! Lol). Put that with a mission, and it's telling us we are to be under the same mission. It doesn't sound so bad now, huh? Now to come up with the mission for your marriage, that is a team exercise. It is not up to you or your husband to solely come up with the mission for a marriage that belongs to the both of you.

You should both come to the table and decide, hey, this is our mission statement, and these are our fundamental values. You have input and value in these major decisions. Even though we may come to the table and put these things into place, it's easy to forget at times or fall back into old habits. So in my eyes, the purpose of submission is to fall under the same mission. Not necessarily for you to submit to whatever your husband says. That's not submission, it's being controlled and having no voice.

My Pastor says often, God does not call us to be a doormat. He has given us gifts and talents that are of great use in our marriages. We should bring all of them to the table. Everyone on the team should be playing up their strengths. As you lay out the mission and decide that financial strength is a priority for your marriage, if you both decide that you, the wife, are better at finances than your husband, then that may be where you dominate (meaning set the ground rules and keep things in decency and order, not control the purse strings). You both can make these decisions. As both of you submit to the marriage mission, you allow your husband to be a leader in your home. Your husband *should* be submitting to God's mission and authority in and over your home.

We are by no means less than or secondary to our husbands. However, our husbands should be our covering. One of their main priorities should be protecting us and also protecting the marriage. Allow him the space and grace to do that (remember he's not perfect and will make mistakes from time to time, it doesn't mean that you need to snatch his title as leader). Ask yourself, what's so bad if your husband is leading over and protecting the guidelines and values that the both of you deemed important? It's not his way or the high way situation (Nah.)

Something that had to happen for me to be even remotely comfortable with submission and my husband being a leader in our marriage was that I had to trust his judgment and relationship with the Lord. I needed to know who he was consulting with when it came down to making decisions for our team. If I'm to trust you to lead us to victory, I don't want you consulting with a friend who has never been married about our difficult decisions. He can discuss things with his friends, but when it comes to making a decision, I want the ultimate consultation to be with God. This is not to say that my husband's relationship with God is perfect. This is one of those progress over perfection, which goes a long way in situations. And I couldn't approach it with an arm crossed. You better be talking to God, Lol (I know, I know, it's hard). I had to do my prayer work, and I had to pray that God would insert himself into his life in a way that my husband couldn't deny that He was the head of his life and decisions.

This is another look in the mirror moment, if we want our husbands to have a flourishing relationship with God, we have to match that energy. What does our relationship with God look like? Are we showing up for our relationship with God before we expect and demand our husbands to have a relationship with God? Again, ladies, it starts with us, and we often have to check ourselves first! If I can trust that my husband is consulting God and taking time to pray before making big decisions, I can trust him as a leader of the most important team I've ever been a part of.

This also means that as the leader (clutch your pears here, Lol), sometimes our husbands' decisions won't be the best ones. It's not helpful to complain and pout or say, *"I told you so."* It's not our job to point out how hard or far he fell. Believe that if you trusted your husband to lead and he fell flat, he's already feeling pretty bad about it. I'm not saying you can't express your feelings, but be mindful of his feelings too.

You don't want him to feel like he can't be trusted ever again or worse, that you aren't to be trusted with his raw emotions. This goes back to being his friend at times. If your friend made a mistake and came to you feeling broken and bruised, I highly doubt you would kick them while they were down. Give your husband that same white-glove treatment at the moment. Great leaders aren't born, they're developed. And even if your husband has been married before, he's never been married to you before. This is a new(er) role for him. Even if you've been married for a while, you aren't the same person you were when you first got married, so he's constantly learning you as a teammate. Give him the grace to grow.

When it gets hard to submit to the mission of your household, pray. I know it sounds very cliché, but hear me out. I've never had a prayer return to me void. It's either going to provide clarity, soften your heart toward the mission or show you how to softly approach your husband so that your thoughts can be seen as loving correction/advice/planning versus an attack. You never want to approach anything in your marriage in an *"I know best"* manner (I know how hard this is because I feel like I know the best a lot, Lol). However, think about if your husband often approached you with an *"I know best"* attitude. Wouldn't that make you feel diminished or less than in some way? I would never want to make my husband feel like that intentionally.

When I need to approach my husband, the best outcomes are always when I pray first. It takes some of the fire and possibly aggression out of my tone. Trust me, this is not in my own strength. What I do know is, no one wants to be made to feel less. Especially not a man who is attempting to lead his family. Even if all you have time to do is stop and whisper a *"help me figure this out, Lord."* Do that. It's better than flying off the handle with no plan because we feel like our husbands are wrong. It comes down to checking our egos at the door and checking in with God before communicating with our spouse.

Another helpful tip is to view your husband as your gift from God. Listen, I know more than anyone that it's hard to see your husband as a gift through his faults, but do your faults stop you from feeling like his most prized possession? I'm going to take a wild guess and say no. There are many days where I am feeling as unstoppable as Beyoncé on that Coachella stage, but in those moments, I still know I'm not perfect. Lol. The thing is, we are both gifts, imperfections and all.

No one is perfect, but we were joined together for a reason. Something one of my friends Rhea Plummer (who is quoted in the wives corner of this book) says often is, the marriage is bigger than just the two of you. There is a purpose in the union. Besides just being in a loving, fulfilling relationship, some lives will be touched and possibly even changed because of your marriage. If you didn't know, marriage is a ministry. It is your first ministry. When you walk outside of your home (with or without your husband), you are ministering to others through the way you speak, treat, and work with your husband.

The mission that you two are working towards or working in is serving more than just the two of you, no matter how big or small. When you feel like you're in a rut and you can't seem to see the beauty in your spouse or the marriage for that matter, take a minute and think about the ways your life would be different if your spouse suddenly were no longer there. How would your everyday life change? When my therapist asked me that question, it took my breath away. It seems simple, but I had never really thought about it like that. I thought that I was not taking my husband for granted. But if I'm being honest and in retrospect I did take him for granted a bit.

As I mentioned earlier, I often operated in an *"I can do for myself attitude."* (even typing that out is hard to stomach). Who would want to live with someone who was acting as if they could do everything themselves? Not I! I took pride myself in my presence being missed when I'm not home. So then how could I walk around and act as if my life partner, my MVP, was disposable? And not based on something he had personally done to our family or me. I had to get real with myself, while I had a front-row seat at the single mom life in my early years, that is not my struggle. My husband is here AND is present. While I am very capable of taking care of myself if I needed to, I don't want to. If my husband decided to get up, walk out, and never return, my life would be drastically different and not for the better. Wow. Let that sink in. Yes, I can do it for myself, but what if I really had to. It's not such a pretty picture to imagine. I don't even want to imagine it. So who was I serving by putting on this hard exterior? Who was benefitting?

No one. Not one person. I had to realize I was wearing someone else's struggle that didn't even fit well. My therapist helped me realize it is a defense mechanism for someone who has a fear of rejection. I will *"reject"* you before you have the chance to reject me. There was no threat of rejection from my husband. I wasn't literally walking around rejecting him day in and day out, but my attitude toward him and our marriage were one of being halfway in and halfway out mentally. You know that I need to keep some stuff to myself and mentally prepare for that doomed day, just in case I need to escape.

Why mentally put yourself through those scenarios when they may never play out for you? You're wasting time and energy on the negativity that may never show up in your marriage. There is no room for that in a flourishing marriage. You're either going to give it 100%, or you're living on edge waiting for the other shoe to drop. If you're living in that state, are you allowing yourself to truly enjoy where you are? There's this Podcast I love and listen to regularly called *"Love Maaden."* The host Maaden (who is also quoted in the wives corner), had an episode with her husband where she talks about giving yourself fully in your marriage. Because why not? What is the purpose in holding back some of yourself? What are you holding it back for? It sounds silly when you think about it. Like yea, I'm going to hold back this extra nice part from him to show him he can't get all of me! Girl!!!!! Why?! Lol. When I really sat back and thought about the giving of myself fully, it resonated with me and had me in deep thought. I recognized that *"holding back"* trait in myself right away. I wasn't giving my full self away in this union, where I should be 100% in. And if I'm honest with myself, anything less than my best is a disservice to my husband and me. Why not give yourself fully to your husband and marriage?

What are you holding back for? For me and maybe for you as well, it requires a full relearning when it comes to romantic relationships. Somewhere somehow, I got the idea that it was weak to give my whole self, and I had to reserve some for myself. But if you're anything like me in this area, ask yourself this question. Does giving yourself fully to your husband take away from your self-worth or self-love you give yourself? The honest answer for myself was no. I still have plenty to give myself, and I had more because being more open and honest with my husband lent him to be more open with me (without us even discussing this). The overflow of love I was getting in that area of my life gave me more gas for loving and pouring into myself (go figure). It is such a freeing feeling! (Not feeling like I have to keep something in the back tuck just in case), Just in case, what?! to embarrass me? This man has seen me give birth to two babies, in two different ways, neither one pretty. I think we're past the stage of a little embarrassment. Give fully because the investment is beyond worth it.

There is no human relationship closer than marriage. Yes, your nuclear family birthed and formed you. Yes, your children were formed inside of you and are literally of your flesh, but these people will always have their own lives to go out and live outside of you. Your husband is your *partner* through all of life's phases. Who are you reserving yourself for? Is there another person you believe you'll be able to give to in this capacity? And if, God forbid your marriage was to fail, would you want it to fail and you feel like you didn't give it all you had? It is not a light switch you just turn on, and then boom, you're living and giving in entirely to your marriage. It's a daily decision that you make to show up fully, completely invested, give all your love, have deep conversations, show love without holding back, and provide safe spaces for both of you to be authentically yourself.

How does this tie into submission, you might ask? I'm glad you asked. If we're honest, the issue some of us may have with submission is giving ourselves to another person or entity to better the whole and not self. It doesn't sound pretty, but it's true. We millennial women often feel like self-preservation first. We often think and hear, if we don't take care of ourselves, who else will? While that might be true, it doesn't mean that we can't both put our all into the marriage we've vowed to be committed to and take care of ourselves. We can take care of ourselves by showing up fully and not shrinking under the title submission. Submission doesn't call us to be less than who we are for the greater good. It calls us to be all of who we are so that we are represented in the mission we're going to stand our marriage on! The idea that under submission, we have no voice is simply not true if done right. If a part of your marriage values is personal growth for the two parts that make up the whole, then personal development for both you and your husband is a part of your marital mission. It's up to you to speak up and make that a priority when you're discussing the values and ideals that will reside in your marriage. Don't forget we wives contribute to this mission we're submitting to. Show up, speak up and then stand on what you both have collectively decided will be your rock in marriage.

While we're talking about giving ourselves fully and freely joining completely with our husbands, we have to assume positive intent regarding the one we've trusted with our hearts. If we cannot release ourselves fully to the person we've chosen to join our lives with and possibly procreate with, what are we saying about ourselves and our decision-making? Trust him, release yourself to him and always give him the benefit of the doubt. Because of the world we live in, I know that someone is always operating out of the best interest for you is hard. As someone who often airs on the side of caution when trusting people, it's easy to have the *"what if"* or *"just in case"* attitude. But again, we could be over-preparing for a war that is never going to happen.

I say all that to say grace goes a long way, and just because your husband may make mistakes sometimes, still show up as his biggest cheerleader. You're both wearing multiple hats and playing duplicate roles sometimes. The key is to do it in love, even when it's hard. If he's leading in love and you're supporting in love, the odds are in your favor!

Words From A Wise Wife

"*Acceptance is Key! We often want to change our spouses into who we want them to be, but in essence, we need to accept them for who God created them to be.*"

-Jamice Holley, MDIV, LGPC, NCC
Art of Becoming, LLC
Married 10 years

Reflection

1. Make a list of all the ways your husband makes your life better. Please find a way to let him in on this list nicely. You can write in a just because card or read it aloud to him during date night.

_____

_____

_____

_____

_____

_____

_____

_____

_____

_____

_____

_____

_____

2. Give your husband a just because gift. It doesn't have to be expensive, just thoughtful and with no motive of receiving anything from him in return.

_____

_____

_____

_____

_____

_____

3. Jot down some of your dreams that include your husband. Now share this list of dreams with him. It will be nice for him to know that some of your dreams include him.

_____

_____

_____

_____

_____

_____

_____

_____

_____

_____

4. How can you put loving your husband into action this week? Make a plan and then do it.

_____

_____

_____

_____

_____

_____

_____

_____

_____

_____

_____

_____

_____

Words From A Wise Wife

"*Your husband wants to be loved just as you do. Often, we put such a high expectation on our husbands fulfilling and meeting our needs that we forget **their** desires, needs, and wants, that we forget about them. Love your husband just as you want to be loved.*"

-Jamice Holley, MDIV, LGPC, NCC
Art of Becoming, LLC
Married 10 years

Reflection

1. How would you rate the prayer in your marriage currently?

_____

_____

_____

_____

_____

_____

_____

_____

_____

_____

_____

2. What do you think would take prayer in your marriage from the number it is right now to a 10 (frequency, intention)?

_____

_____

_____

_____

_____

_____

_____

3. Do you prioritize praying with and for your husband?

_____

_____

_____

_____

_____

_____

_____

_____

_____

4. Ask your husband how you can pray for him today and list it out here. Commit to praying for these things for a week straight.

_____

_____

_____

_____

_____

_____

_____

5. Allow your husband to pray for you by letting him know where you would like him to stand in the gap for you. Give him 3 prayer points for you tonight.

_____

_____

_____

_____

_____

_____

_____

_____

_____

6. Start a prayer box for your marriage with your husband. Both of you talk over something you want to see in and for your marriage in the upcoming year. Write those things down and place them in a box with a lid (we use an old watch box). Pray over this box often. Once your year is up, open the box and see how God has moved in your marriage.

_____

_____

_____

_____

_____

_____

_____

_____

_____

_____

_____

_____

_____

Words From A Wise Wife

"*Always assume positive intent. This is the practice of starting from the idea that your partner meant well or was doing his best, no matter how it may have come across to you. Your husband is the man that has chosen to spend his life with you as partners, and you two are on the same team. He loves you and has your best interest at heart.*

When you misunderstand or miscommunicate, be mindful to listen intently, keep an open mind, lead with love, and assume positive intent. If you are not able to do that at the moment, that's okay. That being said, it's wise to step away from the situation until you are both able and willing to meet one another with love and grace".

-Maaden Eshete Jones
Wife, Mother, and Creator of Love, Maaden
Married 6 years

Pray Like Your Marriage

DEPENDS ON IT

For some of us, prayer comes easy and for others, well…
it just doesn't. I had been a part of the other group for a
long time, and to be transparent, there are still times when I
don't know where to start or exactly what I want to say in
prayer. What I do know, without any hesitation or doubt, is
that prayer changes things. Knowing that prayer is not
optional in my life or in my marriage. Now the prayers may
be a little shaky, lol, but I'm always looking for ways to
design my prayer life into what I need in the season I'm in.

Trying to figure out how to fit in real prayer time in your
life starts by figuring out when you can get some free,
uninterrupted quiet time. We talked about finding quiet
time for you to do some of the things you need to recharge
yourself. Maybe you might start that quiet time off with
prayer or devotional time. The goal should be that you are
alone, electronic devices aside, tv off, and able to really
commit to your conversation time with God (because prayer
is a 2-way street).

Many of us grew up with quick prayers here and there,
thanks to God for opening my eyes, thank God for getting
me to work safely, thank God for this meal, and while all of

that is great, God wants to spend real quality time with us. He is not some object that we should just be running past all day. If we're relying on God for all things all day, we should be able to carve out some alone time with Him to release and receive what He has for us at that moment. If you're anything like me, it may be hard to quiet your mind even if you've removed all the outside distractions.

I have found that writing and, more specifically, writing out my prayers in the SOAP method has helped me tremendously. What's the SOAP method? I'm glad you asked, lol. SOAP is an acronym that stands for *scripture, observation, application, and prayer.* You write the letters out vertically, leaving yourself enough space to write in between each letter. This helps to provide some focus and put my prayers down on paper somewhere. Sometimes I do this while I listen to worship music, which can help me feel like I'm writing God is talking.

During this book-writing process, I have used the SOAP method of prayer many mornings to really sit still and ask God to give me the words (so know the words in this book didn't just come from me, okay?! Lol). On those mornings when I have no idea what I'll pour out on the paper, I go to God in prayer first and ask Him what he would like me to say, and like clockwork, He provides (He's the real MVP). The SOAP method isn't always necessary or maybe just isn't for you. Sometimes you may just want to get down on your knees and cry out. Whatever method you use, the key is to USE it. I used to use my alone time in the car as prayer time, and nothing is wrong with that, but if I'm driving, I'm not giving God all of my attention because I have to make sure I'm driving safely, I can't close my eyes and allow the spirit to speak in the car. While car prayer is good and not wrong, I couldn't use it as my only form of prayer.

I knew I needed to give my prayer life some real attention, and when I may skip a day of uninterrupted quiet time with God, I notice a difference. Give God some of your time daily and watch him change your life, and when you insert prayers about your marriage, He'll change that too. Something that I wanted to introduce to my marriage a few years ago was prayer together. With different schedules and activities, it was hard to figure out what would work for us. We don't go to bed at the same time every night, and I'm up before my husband almost daily.

Once I voiced that this was something important I wanted to do with my husband, we had to come together and figure out what would work for us, us being the keyword (not what was working for the other couples in their marriage ministry). We decided a few years ago that before either of us leaves the house, we would join hands or touch in some way and pray. These prayers aren't hours long, nor my only prayer for the day, but they are our way of approaching God together and asking Him to bless and protect us before we leave each other's presence. It's a time to physically embrace one another and go to the throne of God together. While they are quick prayers, they are impactful. We've been doing this for a while now, so it has become a part of our routine. I may have started it, but now if my husband is leaving out, he will come and find me so we can pray together even if I'm asleep in the bed. See what happened here? There was something I wanted to introduce to the marriage. I communicated my want, and we figured out how it could work for us together, and then sometimes I take the lead on it to make sure it's getting done. It's important to show up to God together as a united front sometimes.

Asking God to bless and keep you together.

Together is powerful.

Matthew 18:20 tells us,

"For where two or three gather in my name,
there am I with them."

I can only imagine how the heart of God smiles when a married couple shows up to commune with Him together. This is also a great practice for your children to see. They may not get it if they are young, but prayer will soon become a natural part of their lives in just watching what mommy and daddy are doing. We started doing this when my oldest was very young, and sometimes we even have him lead the prayer. Exercise what you want them to prioritize.

Now, remember how I said we must be careful about who we discuss our marriages with? I know it's difficult when you're trying to keep yourself from flying off the deep end with your husband, and you feel like I need a release so that I don't lose it on this man! I have been there many times, lol! There are different ways to feel released, you can cry and release emotion, you can journal and put your feelings down on paper, close the page and leave them there. I do all of these things depending on the situation or heated fellowship, as some like to call it, lol. One that never comes back void is praying. I know, I know. In the midst of a heated argument, an elegant prayer is not the first thing that comes to mind, but this is a part of being raw and unfiltered with God. He knows we aren't perfect, and he knows when we're sad, mad, or angry. And I don't think he expects us to come to Him every time with grace and elegance.

Sometimes we're just going to be straight up raw and upset. He knows that he made us human and gave us a range of emotions. Take those emotions to Him, cry out to Him, and sometimes those cries to God are going to look like therapy sessions where we're telling Him all the ways our husband did this or that wrong. The kicker and the reason I love to go to God in these situations is that sometimes (okay, a lot of times). He corrects me and shows me the error of my ways. Now at the moment, it's really an ouch or an ahhhh. Like, what do you mean God? Don't you see what he did? Can't you see how he messed this up? Get him in check!! I go on complaining and *"ratting"* on my husband, and I come out corrected, and seeing how I am or who I was in the situation led to the issue. I love it because it softens my approach with my husband almost immediately (and sometimes not immediately, lol). Now let me tell you, I am a recovering grudge holder.

I could hold my attitude for at least a day if I felt like I needed to teach my husband a lesson, but what good was coming from that? I was creating a war zone in what should be our safe zone and soft space. I wasn't winning because I was holding onto feelings that were causing internal stress and anxiety. My husband wasn't winning because he literally felt like he was living with an enemy and a teammate, and our marriage wasn't winning because I wasn't fostering a space where communication and thus forgiveness could live. Again, I ask who was winning here?!

I would say nobody, but in honesty, that's not true. The enemy was winning. If we aren't talking, loving, touching, laughing, we're creating an atmosphere where the enemy can come in and thrive. The longer we allow that atmosphere to linger, the larger crack we are leaving in the door to let the enemy in. I don't know about you, but that thought alone is enough for me to get my act together and let God correct me. Now, I'm not saying that you can't feel your feelings and take some time to cool off, have a shower, and maybe even sleep on it if that's what your mind and spirit needs to be able to effectively approach the situation in love. Still, we should not be *"icing"* our husbands out for days at a time, trying to make him pay for something we (he lol) did wrong.

I promise no matter how bad you think whatever he did was, if you take it to God in prayer, He'll either show you where you made it difficult for him to win in the situation or equip you to deal with the wrongdoing effectively. Don't be afraid of the correction from God. I know many of us (emphasis on us because whew, lol) feel like we're never wrong, but God knows us better than we know ourselves and honey… Sometimes it is us. A huge part of prosperous prayer life in your marriage is knowing what your husband needs, not only for himself but also within your marriage.

The way you figure this out is simply to ask (there goes that communication again). If you're anything like me, you may feel like sometimes being direct and just asking isn't as *"nice,"* or it takes the element of thoughtfulness out of it. While that may be true, those things are not as important as knowing what the key issues are or what exactly your husband needs at the moment. When you first ask your husband this, it may catch him off guard because he may not readily know what he needs at the moment. Allow him time to think about it, but follow back up.

That shows him that you are just as serious about his needs as you are about your own, you aren't just asking to ask, but you want to support and pray for him. This gesture alone will mean a lot to him, but keep it up. Continue to check-in and continue to take it to the Lord in prayer and watch God work. Sometimes you'll be standing in the gap for your husband on the days when he forgets or simply doesn't have enough strength to pray for himself. Also, you're living out an example of what it would look like for him to pray for you. You want your husband to start praying more? You start first. You want your husband to have a better prayer life; you start first. Model what that might look like and watch for those small changes to occur. Like I've said in other sections, you can't stay close to a fire and not get warm. In this case, you are the fire. You are the most immediate, living example to your husband. Use your influence well. Wife, I'm asking you to pray like your marriage depends on it because it does.

No Idols:
*"Where your treasure is,
there will your heart be also."*
Matthew" 6:21

In the life and times of social media, *"couple goals"* is annoyingly popular. Please, I beg of you, to rid yourself of any couple goals you may be knowingly and unknowingly carrying around. I'm sure you've heard time and time again, people only show you what they want you to know, their highlight reel.

You will never know;

- *What that couple really deals with behind closed doors and/or.*
- *What they had to go through to get to space they are currently in.*

Some things that some couples have had to endure would never work for you and your husband. Some couples can show up and show out together and then go home to separate bedrooms (I don't know about you, but that would never work for me). Never covet the show that someone else is performing without having the entire script. You and your husband are writing your love story, and while I'll always advocate having a mentor couple, that is not saying to try to emulate them. Taking and digesting advice (especially marital advice) is like eating a fish that is not filleted. Eat the meat of the fish (take what is useful and good for you), spit out the bones (get rid of the parts that do not serve the two of you).

Just because someone offers advice, as good as it may be, it doesn't mean that you have to follow it to the end. If you are not careful, you will develop idols when it comes to marriage. *"If only we could do this like them; if only he would look at me the way blank looks at her."* The danger in that is vast. An idol can be defined as an object of worship or adoration. Before you know it, you can become so infatuated with an object or person that you're no longer living the life or, in this case, the marriage you want, and more importantly, that was designed for you. You're simply trying to recreate whatever it is you're enthralled with. You're doing yourself a disservice at life trying to live it like someone you're not.

The gratification you may experience by doing this is temporary. Make a list of who comes to mind when you think of couple/marriage goals. After the list is complete, go through it and draw a line through all of the names. Physically cross it out (you'd be surprised at the role physically doing something plays on the mental). Crossing out these items on this list signifies you're putting them to rest. They may be nice people, but they are not you or your husband. What would make you and your husband your own couple goals? Write that list out, go through it and decide what actually serves you in this marriage. Now that you have a list get to becoming your own couple goals in real life!

Think about what you thought marriage was before being married. However pretty or ugly the image of marriage was to you before you entered it, I want you to redefine that image. Whenever you think of the word marriage, put your team name in front of it. When I think of my husband and me as *"Team Cook,"* it makes our marriage unique and personal to my husband and me. I wouldn't impersonate anyone to create a Cook Marriage because they are not a Cook (even if they have the same last name, they aren't Shanice and Steven). I want you to make your marriage that personal to you every time you think about it.

That will cause you to redefine what you thought marriage was. And because none of us is perfect, there will be things in your marriage that you want to adjust or change. That is why you have team meetings and team-building events. No team just comes together, and with no extra work, practice or engagement, starts winning championships. Winning teams work hard to be winning teams. Think about how exhausting it might be to be married to someone who constantly looked to outside influence for the type of marriage or partner they wanted you to be. Imagine adjusting yourself to fit a stereotype or image your husband wanted you to be based on a movie or show.

You make that adjustment, and then he finds some other idol that he wants you to immolate. Not only do you begin to lose who you are as a person, but how can you keep up? That's unrealistic and unhealthy. If this is something that you are struggling with from your husband, I encourage you to sit him down and ask him what he desires for himself, outside influence. Suppose you are the one fixated on outside influences, back away from the images you're consumed with, and concentrate on the best parts of you and your spouse. Figure out how you can create an environment where the best interests of both of you can flourish, not someone else. If you're lost on where to start figuring out the core values of your home team, I would highly recommend marriage enrichment participation.

I want to spend a little time on marriage enrichment. Many people think that marriage enrichment equals counseling or is super expensive. While counseling may be a part of marriage enrichment, it's not what it is in totality. It could be marriage ministry with your church, seminars, marriage retreats, books, podcasts, or small group participation with other married couples. Depending on what you decide to take part in for your marriage, the cost will vary, but the payoff is great. These kinds of activities lead to conversations you don't necessarily have day-by-day in your home. They provide a space where it's safe to open up deeply with your husband and receive rich encouragement from professionals or other married couples.

I've never attended a retreat, seminar, or even marriage ministry where I didn't come out feeling better than before we started. We've been doing marriage enrichment in different forms since day one, and I'll tell you, it's something I always look forward to. I spoke on having the tools to use before you actually need them. It's always great to find out how your spouse feels about you and the marriage when things are going well. Again, this may be the fuel you need to push past some of the storms that await you in the future. If you know how much you and your marriage mean to your husband before you enter the storm, it's easier to hold hands and approach the storm together with the mindset that it's you and him against the storm, not you vs him. Remember, the same team, the same goal.

If you know me personally, you will know that my husband and I host an annual marriage retreat. The retreat was born out of my desire to attend one locally that didn't break the bank and take away from what we could afford to do for just the two of us and provided us some time around other married couples to grow and learn. The gem here is if you're looking for something that doesn't exist where you are, you may be called to create it, just saying! While putting on this retreat is by no means easy, but it is so rewarding to see couples (especially the men) come out on the other side recommitted to their marriage and rejuvenated in their love. When I say I believe in marriage enrichment, I'm really standing behind it 1000% because I've seen its effects in real-time (not just in my marriage). Take the time out to focus on becoming better for one another and together!

Idols don't always come in the form of other people or other marriages; an idol is anything you are revering in excess. It could be the car, your phone, money, or sex. While sex is a major part of marriage, it should not be idolized above the person you are married to. Let's spend a little time here.

Reflection

AFFIRMATION:
YOUR MARRIAGE DESERVES A
VIBRANT SEX LIFE!

1. If life was not in the way, how many times would you and
   your husband have sex per week?

_____

_____

_____

_____

_____

_____

_____

_____

_____

_____

_____

_____

2. What can you and your husband do to lighten the load so that you are enjoying sex with each other more often? Communicate to your husband how he can assist in this area; I'm sure he'll be willing to do what he must☺.

_____

_____

_____

_____

_____

_____

_____

3. Sex should be FUN! What can you do to increase the excitement in your lovemaking with your husband?

_____

_____

_____

_____

_____

_____

_____

_____

_____

4. Get real! Set aside some time to talk sex with your husband (not while in the act). Ask him if there are things you can do to improve your marriage's sex life.

_____

_____

_____

_____

_____

_____

5. Figure out when you feel the best during sex. Maybe it's taking a shower and moisturizing first. Commit to making yourself feel good before sex as often as possible. When we feel good about ourselves first, we're released to fully enjoy the moment with our husbands instead of worrying about any hang-ups we may have.

_____

_____

_____

_____

_____

_____

Words From A Wise Wife

"*Sex between married couples is a beautiful gift from God. Never use it as a weapon or as a punishment.*"

-Dr. Frances "Toni" Draper,
Pastor, Freedom Temple AME Zion Church
Author, No Ordinary Hookup: The Courtship of
Vashti and Carl Murphy (1915-1916)
Married 47 years

Keeping It

SEXY

Before marriage, I believe most people think once you get married, it will be on and popping regularly. While at times it is, it will probably be hot and steamy in some seasons, and in others, it will be something that happens but not necessarily mind-blowing. God created sex to be equally enjoyable to both the husband and the wife and not just for procreating. Those two statements are realizations that can change your sex life. It's not a method just to get your husband to be nicer, or when you decide you're ready for kids, a way to get them.

That is the closest physical interaction you can have with another human. The one thing only you and your husband can share that you share with no one else is sex. You are physically letting him enter your space. This should be a priority to both of you as it increases intimacy and closeness outside of the bedroom. I am a woman, so I understand it takes more than a look for us to be ready and switch into sexy, take me now mode. We started this book by talking about ourselves.

Let me give you a word of advice that I received early in my marriage. The better you feel about yourself at the moment, the better your sexual experience will be. If you have baby spit up on you and your hair is all over your head, you're probably not going to feel like a goddess if your husband nudges you for some one-on-one time. While I'm not an advocate of saying no to your husband (do what works for your marriage), I am a big advocate of the 'give me a second' antics. We, women, need a second to get our sexiness in order; otherwise, our minds will be everywhere but there in the bed or floor (hey, sometimes you have to switch it up, lol) with our husband.

Take that second to shower, shave, put on some smell goods, brush your hair up, and maybe slip on some lingerie and a lip! I know lingerie is not everyone's cup of tea, or you see it as a waste, but I'll tell you if it helps you feel good, no matter how quick it comes off, it is not a waste. It's just like not feeling well, but dressing up anyway. Eventually, your attitude catches up with your physical appearance, and you begin to feel better about yourself.

Once I feel good about myself, I'm free to jump in and enjoy the experience with my husband. That's exactly what it should be for us, wives, an experience. You should want to be present with him and enjoy the time set aside just for the two of you. If it's something both of you are enjoying and it's creating a closeness for you, you'll be less likely to continue to put it off and use it as a bargaining tool.

The Bible tells us in **1 Corinthians 7:5-7** *that in marriage, we should not withhold sex from one another unless both have agreed to fast but then to come back together so that neither will be tempted.*

I don't think we should move out of fear of our husbands being tempted. I believe that we as women should figure out what works for us and what we like to crave the intimacy and closeness sex brings. Included in this is having conversations (yes, more than one because things change) about what you desire to fulfill in that space.

Notice I said the two of you. Pornography does more harm than good, in my opinion. You are watching actors put on a show. It is not real life. Then you end up trying to reenact what you've watched, and you could be hurting one another, yourself, and it's not even what the other person wants. The best way to figure it out is to talk to each other, not your friends or family but each other. I know it's not necessarily sexy to talk about sex right before or during it; however, if you set aside time and talk about it when sex isn't on the table, it is helpful.

You can really lay down what works and what doesn't. Communicate that when you're considered during the act, he can get the best from you. I'll give you an example, one of my *"rules"* early in our marriage was don't come home late after being out with your friends and wake me up for what you think is about to be a *"wild good time."* It's not a good time for me. It's not fair to me to be woken up and then immediately have to spring into action. Having the conversation ahead of time before being in the act allowed my husband to see my perspective. It kept me from saying *"no"* to, him which can lead to feelings of rejection and then having to go along to get along being resentful the following day. Win-win! Communication goes a long way in the bedroom!

Now that you're married and sex is *"legal"* and readily available, the allure of it can fade. How do you keep the spark? I can think of many ways, including the communication I suggested above. But also, make it fun! That is your husband, and there is a lot of sex to be had; make it spicy and fun. This is your person. Switching locations can introduce excitement, and you don't have to wait for your annual vacation for this. You can have a staycation or just switch it from the bedroom to the living room (if there are no kids around).

New wig, new lingerie, it could be simply improving your atmosphere by lighting candles and turning on music. Again, this goes back to communicating. Discuss some things that both of you would like to see go down in that space and then figure out how to make your intimate experience exciting for the two of you. Once sex is something you have a mutual understanding and appreciation for, it will be easier to put on your radar even when seasons aren't as fiery as they once were (babies change things for sure!). And ladies, as my Pastor said in the Wise Wives Corner above, remember never to use sex as a tool of control or punishment. It will be hard to redirect it to a place of fun and connection in the future.

Often, people intertwine sex and intimacy, and while one can lead to the other, they are not the same thing. Intimacy will, more often than not, create an atmosphere for sex to be more enjoyable. When we feel seen, heard, and understood, we are also more open to being physically close with our husbands. If we've been apart all day and have not even had a moment to check in until the evening when he comes into the bedroom and starts rubbing on us, we're more likely to fake sleep (don't pretend as you've never been there, lol).

When my husband is checking in with my emotions and mental state and makes time for us to communicate about how I'm feeling about anything (not just sex), he sets the stage for whatever might occur later. I want to feel like sex is the icing on the cake, not the batter. Intimacy is often broken down by marital experts in definition as *"in to me see."* When being intimate, you give your husband a picture or deep understanding of what's going on inside your thoughts, feelings, and possibly desires.

Dictionary.com **defines intimacy as**
"A close familial and usually affectionate or loving personal relationship with another person or group."
Also, *"a close association with or detailed knowledge or deep understanding."*

The common thread is familial. To be intimate with one another means that you are becoming close(r), and you become close by making the time to open up with one another. For that to happen, both parties should remain curious about the other and probe your partner with those open-ended questions we talked about earlier. A great tool to use for open and honest conversations are conversation cards or table talk topics (you can search amazon for conversation cards, there are many on the market currently). Having these conversation prompts is excellent because they may pose questions you've never thought of and introduce a new layer of intimacy that you wouldn't have come up with independently.

I love to introduce conversation cards during date nights in which we always end up sharing a deep thought and/or a laugh that makes us feel closer at the end. Keep in mind that if you're inquiring, you want to make sure you're giving him your full attention when he's sharing. You have to ensure the other partner feels safe when sharing, or the sharing will be far and few between, if at all. If you do notice some hesitation or complete withholding, ask him why. That is also a level of intimacy, breaking down the barriers that hold either one of you back from sharing your innermost self with the other.

You may be the one withholding; maybe you feel like he won't take you seriously or may think your feelings are insignificant. You should find the right time (timing is everything, don't attempt to have this conversation as soon as he walks in the door) to explore what may be blocking your ability to be fully transparent with your husband. Sex and intimacy are a big part of marriage. It's said that they are the thermostat for the relationship. If you lack in that area, some other issues are likely keeping you from wanting to be intimate and physical with your husband. Use some of the tools in this book to dig deep and get to the bottom of it. If you've done the diagnostic, and that is not the case, girl! What are you waiting for? Get naked both literally and figuratively with your man!

Reflection

1. What is a promise that you can make to yourself that will have you show up as a better friend to yourself first and then your husband (*If you think of more than one, include them all*)

_____

_____

_____

_____

_____

_____

_____

_____

_____

_____

_____

_____

_____

2. Is there anything in your vows that you can remember promising at the alter you have not tapped into that you can implement today?

_____

_____

_____

_____

_____

_____

3. Verbalize to your husband how you intend to support him in a project he has going on.

_____

_____

_____

_____

_____

_____

_____

_____

4. Research a marriage retreat or seminar in your area (there are tons of free conferences and seminars online currently) and plan to register and attend one within the following year. Write your options here.

_____

_____

_____

_____

_____

_____

_____

5. How do you intend to be the best version of yourself, not just for him but also you're your marriage? Use this space for brainstorming, and then communicate this to your husband. This communication will hold you accountable for your word.

_____

_____

_____

_____

_____

_____

_____

Words and Actions

"Thus, also faith by itself, if it does not have works, is dead."
James 2:17

When it comes to your marriage, I want you to not only say you desire to have a great marriage. I want you to live it out every single day. I know that sounds like a lot to have to put forth the effort every day, but what's a lot when it comes to living an inspiring and life-giving life? Imagine being out amongst company and saying the words; we have a great marriage, and your husband is looking confused. Looking at you like, *"whose marriage is she talking about? Not ours, we just finished arguing in the car"* (it happens to the best of us sometimes, lol).

The goal is to be out amongst company and never have to utter those words because it's evident how you're treating and loving each other. Now keep in mind that great doesn't equal perfect. Great is a partnership where both spouses feel, see, take care of, love and fulfill (whatever those things look like to the both of you). A huge part of living out what works for the both of you is identifying what that is and then vocalizing it. That is one of those areas where you have to check in with each other. Just like you check in with yourself about things that are working and aren't working, do that with your husband. Maybe at every quarter, take time to pause and reflect. Ask him, *"babe, what worked really well for you in the marriage this quarter?"* Check-in verbally, don't just go off to your room and journal about what you liked and didn't like. Make it a thing!

Proverbs 18:21 tells us that
"the tongue has the power of life and death."
It is our choice on how we use our tongue,
but no matter how we choose to use it, it has power.

What are we speaking into our marriages and our husbands? When we boldly declare something, we are giving it power, giving it life. Decide with your husband, do we want kids at all, do we want more kids? Do we want to work for corporations outside of the house, or do we want to be entrepreneurs? Do we want to buy a home or rent an apartment? Only both of you should answer these questions without the influence of others because it is both of you who will have to live day in and day out with the results of the decisions you've made. Imagine you decide for your life based on the opinion of a friend. Then, later your friend makes a decision for themselves that is different from what they advised you to do, and you're left living out a life based on a decision you made based on someone else's opinion who has the right to change their mind. Whenever you're making a decision for your household, first take it to the Lord in prayer so that you allow yourself and your husband to hear from God on it. Allow God to show you which way He desires for you to go. Often when we make choices to God, He will either give us confirmation or a nagging feeling that something isn't right.

After you've given time to the decision in prayer, make sure you and your husband are on the same page. If you make sure that both you and your husband are completely bought into the decisions you're making for your life, it's easier to deal with the fallout of it, good or bad. Don't give that kind of power to any person outside of your marriage. Influence is natural, but it's what you do with that influence that matters. Influence should give you something to consider or think about; it shouldn't push you into a decision you wouldn't have made otherwise. Earlier, we discussed knowing who you were as a person.

Once you get married, it's also crucial to know who you and your husband are as a unit. As time goes on, if it comes to a time-sensitive decision, you should be able to speak on behalf of both of you based on the core beliefs and values you both have already discussed and established. That all takes work, which takes us back to faith without works, is dead. It's amazing to have faith that you'll be married until death; those are the impactful words a lot of us said the day we got married, but what work are you putting in to ensure that those words will ring true? Without the work, the faith will fall flat. I remember being newly married and thinking, what works? You mean we won't always naturally feel this high off life?

Unfortunately, as many of us know, the answer to that is no. We know that the same height can be achieved, but how much are we willing to work for it? You have to work at and for it, especially when you introduce careers, children, other family members, friends, layoffs, sickness. These things will come to test you. It's the work you put in when things are *"good"* that will give you the strength to hold on when things get rough. It's not a matter of IF things will get rough. It's a matter of when. This is life! Things are cyclical.

If life was difficult as a single person, add another person to the mix who grew up with different experiences, desires, values. You now have to merge all of that and then deal with what life throws your way. The way to join together and face those crashing waves together is to develop your defense plan ahead of time. If you're approaching the wave and trying to figure out your plan as it approaches, you'll get swept up off your feet amid your plan. And your plans will change as life goes on, and you both also change and grow.

Seasons of life and marriage are fluid; they aren't the same either, so your battle plans won't always be the same. What we don't want is to just say through thickness and thin. We want to show up in thickness and thin. This is why constant communication is imperative. I'm not saying you need to discuss these kinds of things every day. Men aren't going to be eager to have these kinds of discussions all day, every day. But maybe you make sure bi-monthly at date night, you introduce the conversation. Try to make these discussions light and fun so that neither of you dreads it.

You never want to discuss the future and vitality of your marriage to seem like a chore because then neither of you will ever want to do it. If you never want to do it, you'll look up, and years will have passed, and your success plan will be outdated. Give power to your marriage by speaking life into it. Once you've spoken life, then I want you to act and walk in the faith you have in the work you're putting in.

Practical Ways To

COMMUNICATE

When I first got married, and people would preach communication repeatedly, I felt bored with the topic. If we were attending a marriage ministry or conference and I would see it as a topic, I would roll my eyes and cringe. Gosh, everyone just says communicate, communicate, communicate. What else? What are we communicating? I thought people were beating the communication horse to death. What I really wanted to know was the magic sauce for a fun, hot, and romantic marriage? It can't just be communication!

But honestly, communication is just very important! The truth is, a lot of us think we're effectively communicating with our spouse, but we aren't; let that sink in. We can be talking to one another and really saying nothing, or the other could barely be listening. Especially if we've been married for a few years, throw some kids in the mix, and right in front of our eyes, all we could really be doing is have a bunch of hallway conversations. You'd be surprised at the number of people who really don't even know their spouse at all and have become great associates. What is a hallway conversation? You may ask. It is the passing by someone in the hallway at work and asking how are you and not really meaning it? You ask, and they reply fine as you pass each other. No one is really expecting to open up a deep, meaningful conversation as you pass each other in the hallway.

After all of those little conversations with our spouse, are we really tapping into what each other needs or how we're feeling? If you ask your husband how his day was and he answers good, and y'all move on, have you learned anything at all about his day? When he says, *"his day was good."* Ask him what made it good? Are you really interested in the questions you've asked, or are you just on autopilot, and that's a nice thing to ask when he gets home? It's okay to say *'ouch'* right there because I'm sure we've all been guilty of this. People can often tell when someone is asking something out of courtesy or if they're really interested. If I ask you how you are, but my face is buried in my phone, would you feel like I really care how you're doing? If I'm going through something, I'm probably not going to open up and bear my soul with someone who looks preoccupied. I mentioned earlier that we hugely communicate with our body language. When we say one thing and our body shows another thing, what do you think speaks louder? We can say a lot, but if our body isn't following up on what's coming out of our mouths, it is worthless. Your mouth cannot outperform your actions.

The first piece of practical advice I have for you about improving communication is to cut out time to communicate with your whole body entirely. There will be times when it is okay to ask questions while you fold the laundry, like needing to know what time your husband will be home. Asking him how he's feeling is not one of those times. If you're really interested in how your husband is doing, cut out some uninterrupted time where you can put aside all other things, make eye contact, maybe physically connect by holding hands or rubbing his back, and really seem interested in the question you're asking. When you cut out this time to give him your undivided attention, request that he does the same.

Now, let's say you make space for communicating with your whole body, and you ask a deep question, and he replies with one word. I'm going to challenge you to ask a follow-up open-ended question. Meaning, if you ask, *"how are you feeling,"* and he replies, *"great,"* your charge is to follow up with what is making you feel great right now? Or *"what can I do to add to your positive feelings"?* The key is first to communicate that you are really interested in what you're inquiring about and then to be able to indulge in meaningful conversation that you may not get to do during another time of your day.

That is why married people will say date night is so important. It provides space to tune out the distractions from everyday life (chores, kids, tv, phone) and provides a new, fun environment for you to relax and get lost in one another. Tips: don't allow cell phones during date night. You can put on 'do not disturb for all people except your favs,' so if the person who has the kids needs to contact you, they can, but no scrolling and unimportant conversations. That is not just your time together; it's the time your marriage needs to grow. Don't allow the distractions to subtract from that time.

The second piece of practical advice I have for improving communication with your husband is don't allow yourself to discuss important issues about him or your marriage with any other person first. I say person because you can take it to God in prayer and if you're anything like me, talk to yourself about it, lol. Take a second and ask yourself how you would feel if all your husband's friends knew that he couldn't stand that you don't clean your closet regularly, and you had no clue.

Yes, it's a small thing, but it's something you're unaware of. He has shared that with people who can't change it and with people outside of your union who now know something about you and really him, you haven't even had the opportunity to correct it because you have no idea he even cares. Give your husband and your marriage the courtesy of communicating your requests and desires with him first. Please don't leave him out of things that include him, and better yet, allow him to course correct. You could be driving yourself crazy, gossiping *(that's what it is, in all honesty)* about him, and you haven't even given him the space to correct the behavior because you haven't gone to him with the issue.

Third, ladies read this slowly and carefully. If your husband asks you what's wrong and there is really something wrong, be honest. I don't know one woman who has never defaulted to the nothing answer when asked what's wrong, but ladies, spoiler alert. Your husband is asking what's wrong because it is evident something is wrong! I know for myself I would say nothing to avoid an argument at the moment, but the moment was already tainted with the attitude that nudged my husband to ask me what's wrong. We aren't really avoiding or hiding anything by saying nothing.

Now here's a hard truth; we're just telling a bold-faced lie. Something is wrong, and instead of lying about it, we should find a productive way to express what has our feathers ruffled. It's better to figure out how to gently approach the issue so that you don't make matters worse by avoiding it. Sometimes, when asked, you may not have the words to express exactly how you feel. What may be helpful in those moments is to let him know you need a second to process your thoughts before spewing them out to him. That way, you have a moment to get your thoughts together and maybe your attitude, lol, and you aren't frustrating your husband by clearly hiding what has you upset. Open and honest communication is always the goal, and we can't get there if we aren't willing to share.

The fourth and final practical piece of communication is Advice. Find fun ways to have difficult conversations. You may hear a lot of people talk about the sandwich method, and it is beneficial. If you've never heard of the sandwich method, it's when you sandwich the least exciting part of your conversation between two great things. For example, if I want to approach my husband about me feeling like he spends too much time on his phone, I could sandwich it in this way; Babe, you are such an amazing spouse. I just can't get enough of you! Lately, I've noticed you spend a lot of time on your cell phone, and I want to spend more time with you with no distractions. What do you think about having *"no phone hours?"*

I could then finish the conversation by saying, 'I'm so glad I get married to someone like you, who I love spending time with.' This may seem like a lot, but if you approach this same scenario in a more abrasive way, you may get a completely different outcome. Imagine the same issue, but this time you say, *"UGH, you're always on that annoying phone. You never want to spend quality time with me."* I think you can imagine the response you may get would be completely different. Not only is sandwiching your thoughts an excellent way to express an underlying issue, but you can also set parameters around which you'll have difficult conversations.

Let's say finance is not an area where you shine in marriage, but you need to discuss your finances monthly to get the budget for the month in order. Give yourselves an incentive by saying, 'after our not so *"fun"* money meeting, we will always have a fun date night.' Even if it's a date night in (sans the kids if you have them). So you know the conversation may be difficult or uncomfortable, but you have the date night to look forward to. Caution! Do not take the money conversation (or whatever the difficult conversation is) into the date night. Date night is meant to be enjoyed!

No difficult conversations where love taps and flirting should live! You don't want to taint date nights with negative talk or arguments because then you'll make date night an experience neither you nor your husband wish to partake in for fear of it ending on a sour note. I always say date nights are super important in marriage because when you aren't intentional about carving out uninterrupted downtime with your spouse, everyday life will continue to chip away at the relationship until you don't recognize it anymore. Is it hard to plan and schedule a sitter and make a reservation? If you aren't a planner, maybe. Is it worth it? Every Single Time!

To Counsel or Not

TO COUNSEL

I feel like marriage counseling gets a bad rap. I would say I don't know why, but that's not true. I think I understand why people are reluctant to go to counseling, especially if, at first glance, everything seems to be on the up and up in your marriage. People typically think marriage counseling is the hospital you take your marriage to when it's sick or dying. That's just simply not true, though. My husband and I have led the marriage ministry at our church for several years, and we always say to couples, do you drive your expensive car around forever and ever with no oil change or tune-up? The answer is no, or it would no longer be running.

We should think of our marriages the same way. Suppose we're running our marriages to the ground, of being all the things to other people first and giving our marriage and spouse the junkyard scraps that are leftover. In that case, I can almost guarantee your check engine light is on, and you aren't paying attention. The great thing about going to counseling before you start smelling smoke is that you'll already possess some tools as a couple to pull out the bag once you get to those rough patches. If you get to those rough patches with no road map or tools, you may think it's time to trade in your car (or marriage) for a new one when all you need is maintenance. Maintenance is so much cheaper and less invasive than having to replace a whole vehicle. Counseling is a great way to introduce a non-biased voice of reason. You and your husband are typically emotionally charged when it comes to meaningful conversations. So it may be hard to really hear and understand what the other person is trying to communicate. The counselor should break it down into small, digestible nibbles so you can understand each other better.

I also once heard a great couple's therapist say, the two individuals are not my client, but the marriage is. My job is for the marriage to win, not the wife or the husband. Boom! That's it! We've explored that idea earlier in the marriage. The goal is for the marriage to win. When we're in the midst of the disagreement, it's easy to feel like I'm going to win and get my point across. I'm going to win! But, that attitude is not beneficial to the whole team. You always want to have the team's best interest at heart, and a good counselor should be helping you keep your marriage.

Counseling is a great way to introduce a non-biased voice of reason. You and your husband are typically emotionally charged when it comes to meaningful conversations. So it may be hard to really hear and understand what the other person is trying to communicate. The counselor should break it down into small, digestible nibbles so you can understand each other better. I also once heard a great couple's therapist say, the two individuals are not my client, but the marriage is.

My job is for the marriage to win, not the wife or the husband. Boom! That's it! We've explored that idea earlier in the marriage. The goal is for the marriage to win. When we're in the midst of the disagreement, it's easy to feel like I'm going to win and get my point across. I'm going to win! But, that attitude is not beneficial to the whole team. You always want to have the team's best interest at heart, and a good counselor should be helping you keep that man thing.

It's a great thing to have therapy sessions where you get to discuss and explore things that you aren't sitting at home talking about every day. You may be surprised to find out how your husband is viewing you currently. It could be the encouragement you need that shows you the work you've been silently putting in is paying off, and he sees you! You may also find out some things he doesn't like or appreciate, but that is also good!

Now you have a roadmap of things to keep going with and something to work on. These are conversations that may have never happened otherwise, and now you know exactly where to put your efforts instead of guessing. I don't know about you, but I'd rather use my energy in the places that positively impact my marriage. If my husband has the answer code, please, sir, pass it on over! Counseling can take the guesswork out of many things for us and set us straighter on our road to a healthy, happy marriage! Don't be afraid or ashamed of seeking help from a professional. You can put on a happy face and pretend in a lot of places. Hopefully, your home is not one of them. If some things need to be ironed out, do it! You do not impress anyone (including your husband) by suffering alone in silence. Google the counselor, sis!

Reflection

AFFIRMATION:
I AM WILLING TO DO WHAT I HAVE TO DO TO
LIVE THE MARRIAGE I DESIRE AND DESERVE!

1. What is one concept from this book I am willing to practice regularly to improve the intimacy in my marriage?

_____

_____

_____

_____

_____

_____

_____

_____

_____

_____

_____

_____

2. Three things I realized I could work on and am going to commit to improving are?

_____

_____

_____

_____

_____

_____

_____

_____

3. The area in this book that spoke to me the loudest is?

_____

_____

_____

_____

_____

_____

_____

_____

_____

4. This year as a couple, we are going to get away to…?

_____
_____
_____
_____
_____
_____
_____
_____

5. Can I be a better friend to my husband by…?

_____
_____
_____
_____
_____
_____
_____
_____
_____

Words From A Wise Wife

"If I could offer wives any advice when your husband does something to upset you. Be as honest as possible but also discerning about the time and content of the complaint. When I'm upset with my husband I ask myself 2 questions. One, does it have to be discussed right now or can it wait? Two, is he the problem or is it a trigger from a past relationship or trauma that I've internalized and not yet dealt with? I then approach the issue from a more thought out point of view and so far it's been amazingly beneficial to me!"

-Sethlina Amakye
Entrepreneur of sethlinaamakye.com
Married 10 years

Conclusion

"Be very careful, then, how you live, not as unwise but as wise, making the most of every opportunity, because the days are evil."

Ephesians 5:15-16

This scripture speaks volumes on wisdom. It also lets us know that tomorrow is not promised, and we should never take for granted the opportunities we have to live well and love well today! The days (and some people in today's world) may be evil, trouble may be around the corner, but today we can choose joy and love! We've all heard the phrase, *"when you know better, you do better."* How can we desire to do better without purposefully seeking the knowledge to do better? We have to remain curious about how we can become better people and then ultimately better spouses. As I mentioned before, our marriages are bigger than us. From our families come children who are formed and groomed by watching how we operate and figure things out in the home. A strong foundation is priceless, and what we can provide by being the very best versions of ourselves in our homes every day can lead to a great legacy.

I don't proclaim to be a marriage expert or to know all that is to know on the subject. However, I do know that I enjoy being a lifelong student of love and what it can provide. I also subscribe to each one to teach another. I gain nothing by having a great marriage and keeping all my *"secrets"* to myself. As I learn, I will continuously pay it forward because seeing the benefits of this work is rewarding. It is rewarding not just for me and my marriage, but it is rewarding to see married couples that look like my husband and me, not just making it work because they *"have to"* but making it work because they want to!

During slavery, our people were robbed of the power that resides in the family. They divided us so that we could not conquer. Families were torn apart and isolated because even those outside of us knew how powerful we could be if united. That then turned into messaging that Black Love did not and could not exist. It was (and sometimes still is) rare to see commercial messages with whole black families. Healthy marriage in our community is not something I take lightly.

I speak highly of my husband and our marriage purposefully. I wear our family name as a badge of honor because black love does exist, and we can and have done it well as a community! I want to see us all not merely survive marriage but thrive in it! When you're happy at home, the fallout of that happiness on everything else is massive. I pray that there is something written in this book you were able to learn from, something that made you laugh, made you realize you weren't alone, and finally, something that made you realize that you can have the marriage you deserve and desire. It's all at the end of the work you're willing to put in. Marriage is work, yes. But it is good work!

Marriage ARE YOU DESIGING THE YOU DESERVE?

Visit designingthemarriageyoudeserve.com
to learn about upcoming Marriage retreats and more!

www.ingramcontent.com/pod-product-compliance
Lightning Source LLC
Chambersburg PA
CBHW070042100426
42740CB00013B/2769